Angel

By
Captain Arthur Ray Hawkins, USN (Ret)
With
Louise Bancroft Hawkins

copyright ©2006 by Arthur and Louise Hawkins.
Printed and bound in the United States of America.
All rights reserved. No portion of this book may be reproduced or transmitted in any form or by any means, electronic or mechanical, including photocopying, recording, or by information or storage and retrieval system without the expressed written permission of the author.

Cover Layout:
Ashley Spears
AES Graphics

Trent's Prints & Publishing
Chumuckla, Florida
www.trentsprints.com

Published August 2006
United States of America

ISBN: 1-934035-10-6
ISBN-13: 978-1-934035-10-8

Louise Hawkins
28496 Perdido Pass Dr.
Orange Beach, AL 36561
Hawkinsu@gulftel.com

Table of Contents

Pearl Harbor	1
Winning My Wings	17
My First Kill	31
Mariannas Turkey Shoot	45
The Battle of the Philippine Sea	61
I Have Returned	87
The Philippines	99
Peace Treaty	109
Prisoner of War Flights	113
Civilian	125
Return to the Regular Navy	143
Korea	159
Supersonic Ejection	179
Test Pilot	203
Cold War	213
Deep Draft Command	227
Japan and Vietnam	241
Retirement	257

FOREWORD

This account of memories and stories was written by and about Captain Arthur Ray Hawkins, U.S. Navy (Retired). "Hawk" served with bravery and distinction through the three wars that shaped the latter half of the twentieth century and our lives today. He recounts in intricate detail war experiences from his 31 years in the Navy through World War II, Korea and Vietnam. Hawk was not only a first-hand witness to our history, he helped shape it.

Called "Hawk" by his friends and those who knew him well, he was one of the Navy's most decorated Naval Aviators. He received the Navy's highest award for bravery, the Navy Cross, three times. In addition, he was awarded three Distinguished Flying Crosses, four Air Medals and two Legions of Merit.

His book tells of his actions in the major battles on the Allies' island-hopping march across the Pacific to the Japanese homeland. Harrowing air combat, the rescue of the prisoners of war and the signing of the Japanese peace treaty are just some of the historical milestones he witnessed personally. The movements of Naval Task Forces, play-by-play dog fights and other exciting moments are all captured in the following pages. He has also captured some of the humor that helped the pilots to face the stress of impending combat and, in these pages, we experience that as well, with Hawk.

As a widow, I met and married Hawk some twelve years ago. A very private person, he only talked of his experiences when asked about a specific happening. Because of this, along with his children and grandchildren, I was not aware of the details of his many exploits. Even though his friends had urged him for many years, he had not even begun to write his memoirs and put his story down for posterity.

I did notice though that even this long after World War II, it was not unusual for a letter to arrive almost weekly from a history buff or an autograph collector wanting an autograph or a signed picture. One request came from a lady wanting an autograph on two small pieces of cloth that were to be used in making a quilt that had been in the planning stage since World War I. Sale of the quilt would be donated to the Red Cross, she told me. She sent a long list of the people who, over the years, had signed the pieces of cloth. I was astonished to see such names as Presidents Taft, Wilson and Hoover, Albert Einstein, Winston Churchill, General Pershing, Helen Keller, Bing Crosby, Ernest Hemingway, Clark Gable and others. My husband had been included among such names making me realize that Hawk's wartime accomplishments had made him one of the true heroes of what Tom Brokow called the "Greatest Generation."

It had always been my feeling that the stories of these heroes needed to be told, and I was aware that their ranks were thinning out at a fast pace. I felt that the stories of those who fought to attain and assure our freedom should be preserved for future generations. I knew that many more heroes would be spawned by the current war on terrorism and new printable stories would emerge. The quilt and Mr. Brokow's book provided the catalyst, and I assigned myself the mission of encouraging Hawk to sit down and record his story.

It was not easy to get this humble man to put, in narrative form, what it was like and what he had accomplished during his long Navy career. I promised, resolved and gave him my full cooperation. My assistance may have been small, but I was allowed to select the title of the book, "Angel in the Cockpit." I decided on the title after learning of Hawk's many narrow escapes from death, some of which appeared to have been brought about through divine intervention. With a good tape recorder and Hawk's countless hours, we cut, pasted and printed - wearing out two computers as the work took on manuscript form. I believe we have put together a compelling story, Hawk's story.

 I would like to express my thanks to those who helped with this book. My gratitude to Vice Admiral Jerry Miller USN (Retired), Barbara Martin Lewis for her editing contributions, Marcia Karen Martin for her interviewing and editing, as well as John Crawford and Captain Kenneth Wallace for their helpful memories and anecdotes.

 I know you will enjoy the book.

Louise Bancroft Hawkins

Chapter One

Pearl Harbor

I watched them as they wandered through the museum, young, clean-shaven, freshly scrubbed Naval Air Cadets in their summer whites. They stopped in front of the F6F Hellcat.
"Wow, look at this one," one of them said.
"Not very big, is it?" another challenged.
"It's big enough."
"Not like an F-18."
"Well, no, but it's bigger than a Cessna 150."
They all laughed.
"Can you imagine flying one of these things in actual combat? No over-the-horizon kills with this baby. You had to get eyeball to eyeball."
"What's the sign say about it?" one of the cadets asked.
"I don't know. Let's take a look."

I knew what the sign said. My name is Arthur Ray Hawkins, I am a retired Navy Captain, and as Secretary Treasurer of the Pensacola Naval Air Station Museum, I had approved the sign before it was placed on the easel in front of the plane just inside the rope barrier.

```
            GRUMMAN F6F HELLCAT
     WINGSPAN            42ft 10in
     LENGTH              33ft 10in
     HEIGHT              14ft  5in
     GROSS WT           15,413 lbs
     MAX SPEED             380 MPH
     MAX RANGE               1,530
                POWERPLANT
       PRATT WHITNEY R2800 2,000 HP
                 ARMAMENT
         SIX .50 CALIBER MG W/2400 ROUNDS
```

As the Naval Air Cadets continued their examination of the airplane, they walked around to where I was standing.

"Excuse me, sir," one of them said. He pointed to the airplane. "Are you old enough to remember this plane?"

"Yes," I said.

"I guess it was something in its day, huh?"

"It was," I replied.

One of the cadets found something else of interest, and calling to his friends, led them away. I stood for a moment longer, then went back into my office. I worked for the rest of the day, not realizing it was late until one of the staff stuck his head just inside the door of my office.

"Captain Hawkins, I'll be leaving now. All of the visitors are gone."

"Okay, thanks, Charley, I'll lock up."

I answered a letter from a young history student at the University of Colorado, then I left my office and walked out onto the floor of the 300,000 square foot facility.

There is no more alone feeling in the world than to be the only person in a large museum, surrounded by ghosts of the past.

Angel In The Cockpit

I stopped for a moment to look at the NC-4, the Curtis Seaplane that made the first Atlantic Crossing by air. I had seen pictures of it before it arrived at the museum, but I was not prepared for how large it actually is. As I stood there I thought about her crew, communicating with each other through the ancient gosport and overcoming tremendous odds to land in Lisbon Bay on that summer day in 1919.

There are several other aircraft on display as well, all with their own stories to tell. Then I walked back to the Hellcat, the same airplane I had been examining earlier in the day. One of the cadets had asked if I could remember the Hellcat. I had not given him a complete answer. Not only could I remember it, I had flown it during World War II.

You weren't supposed to do it, and I wouldn't have done it had I not been the only one in the museum at the time. But I climbed up onto the wing, slid back the canopy, and lowered myself into the cockpit. I put my feet on the rudder pedals, wrapped my right hand around the stick, and put my left hand on the quadrant that housed the throttle, prop and mixture levers.

I once read an article that when you remember something, your mind is actually traveling through time, reforming its neurons and synapses to create an exact reconstruction of the original event. I can attest to that, for that is actually what happened as the years and history rolled back for me. Even though I was sitting in a display Hellcat at a museum in present-day Florida, I had, through this "time travel of the mind," returned to 0545 on the morning of the 29th of April 1944. On that morning the USS Cabot (CVL-28), a fast carrier, was steaming with Admiral Marc Mitchner's Task Group 58.2 some 120 miles south of Truk Atoll.

I was existing in two eras. Part of me realized that this was the present, but just as strongly, I could see myself in the earlier time, flipping the toggle switch to activate the starter. There was a high pitched whine as the inertia wheel built up energy followed by the chirp as it engaged, then the coughing rumble, and finally the roar of the big Pratt and Whitney engine.

To me, it seemed as if it had been only a few minutes ago when I was in the ready room with the other pilots, getting briefed for today's mission.

Lt. Commander Robert Winston was not only our squadron commander; he was also CAG, or Commander of the air group. He was a little older than the rest of us, tall, slender, with a pencil-thin moustache and the most piercing eyes I had ever seen. He wasn't much for chewing you out if you messed up. He didn't have to. One disapproving glance from those eyes was all that was needed. Appropriately enough, Winston was the first one of us to shoot down a Japanese plane, and by war's end he would be an Ace.

"Gentlemen," he said. "This is going to be a busy day. We've already launched a morning strike against Truk, and it's on its way to the target. We have a combat air patrol up now, but we expect to be hit by Japanese dive bombers and torpedo planes. That's where we come in. Stewart?"

"Yes, sir?" Stewart answered. Lieutenant Junior Grade James Stewart was commander of the Sixth Division.

"I want your division in position to be first up."

"Yes, sir," Jimmy answered. "Hawk, you'll be first," he said to me.

"Yes sir," I replied, smiling broadly at the opportunity.

"Don't be greedy, Hawk," Frank Hayde teased. "Save some Japs for the rest of us."

Frank Hayde was my closest friend in the squadron, and my roommate.

"Oh, I expect there will be plenty Japs to go around," Winston said. "Pilots, hit the head while you can, then, man your aircraft."

Several of the men took the commander's suggestion, but I had relieved myself just before the briefing, so I went directly up to the deck where I was assisted into the plane by one of the deck crew, or Airedales as they were called. I could barely contain my excitement as he helped me fasten the parachute harness.

I would like to give you a feel for what it is like on a carrier just prior to a launch. It is an amazing overload of the senses to witness hundreds of men dodging whirling propellers as they scurry about among scores of airplanes, some with folded wings, others with their wings already deployed. You *see* a myriad of colorful shirts among the deck crews, each color designating a certain job. You *hear* the deep-throated rumble of engines that are already turning over, the shrill putt-putt of the little tractors that are moving the planes about, and the sounds of the Klaxons, bells, and boatswain's pipe. You *smell* the fuel and oil and hydraulic fluid and the distinct, but indescribable bouquets that waft up from the bowels of the ship through hatches and vents. You *feel* the pitch and roll of the aircraft carrier and you *taste* the salt-spray wind in your face as the vessel is making thirty knots.

I was aware of all of this as one of the launch crew guided me onto the catapult. I had to look along the side of the nose to see my taxi guide, as the nose was too high and too big for me to look directly over it.

Once in position on the catapult I sat for several moments, just waiting, monitoring my gauges . . . oil pressure, cylinder head temperature, manifold pressure, fuel pressure, and generator. When I got the word to go, I didn't want any mechanical malfunction.

Then, there was an increased amount of activity among the deck personnel. Over my radio I received a hasty message from the combat information center.

"Attention all ready aircraft. A flight of enemy torpedo bombers is approaching the fleet from the starboard side. Launch at once and engage."

Every motion the launch officer makes just prior to takeoff is greatly exaggerated. It is a graceful choreography of mime and ballet. They have to do this in order that no signal goes undetected or misinterpreted.

Holding his arm high over his head, the launch officer made a wide circular motion with his hand, then pointed to me. That was a signal for me to go to full power. I moved the throttle and prop lever forward, and as the airplane strained and shook under the stress of maximum RPM, I stood on the brakes, then gave the launch officer a salute.

Dramatically, the launch officer squatted, faced the front of the carrier and pointed toward the end of the deck. The catapult was fired and the Hellcat hurled down the flight deck, moving so fast that all around me was a blur.

The most wonderful thing about memory is that it is not constrained by a specific chronological sequence. I can suspend it at the very point of this take-off, and revisit an earlier time, a more innocent time.

Angel In The Cockpit

<u>The "Z" is for Zavalla Highschool, where I lettered in Basketball</u>

I was born in Zavalla, Texas on December 12, 1922, the youngest of three boys. Zavalla is a small town in the Piney Woods of East Texas and at the time of my birth, sported little more than a barber shop, sawmill, general store, laundromat, a gas station and a post office. The last real excitement was the completion of a new concrete bridge for the highway between Lufkin and Beaumont. My father, Alva M. Hawkins owned the "washeteria" and a rental house in Zavlla Texas. He also had some connection to a local sawmill. He stood six foot four in his stocking feet, weighed over 200 pounds, and was nicknamed Big Hawk. Often, he was a volunteer policeman, and he had earned the respect of the community.

My mother was Gillie B. Russell Hawkins. My childhood friends called her Miss Gillie and she made sure that my two older brothers and I stayed on task with our school work. My brother, Ford, was four years my senior, and Guy was two years older than I.

My best friend was John Crawford and his family lived across the street from us. He was my age and his two older brothers, Floyd and Prentice were about the same ages as my older brothers. John's father ran the only garage/gas station in town and John sometimes helped out by pumping gas. Logging was the major industry in the region and trucks trundled through town all day long carrying long yellow pine logs south for export.

In the late twenties and early thirties, we lived the life of a Norman Rockwell painting. A hot Texas summer day might find a group of us boys stripping down to birthday suits to swim in the cooling waters of a nearby, spring-fed creek, or taking our cane poles to the mill pond to go after catfish. Sometimes we would climb trees and jump to the crown of a nearby sapling to ride it down to the ground as it bent. We also played 'war' with guns made from wood scraps and clothespins shooting rubber bands cut from old inner tubes.

Boyhood Friends (Hawk is third from left)

As country boys often do, we loved to hunt. We didn't care whether it was squirrel, rabbit or deer; we were very good at it. During the depression, our families always welcomed the contribution to the dinner table.

On Saturday nights our family would gather around the big console radio to listen to the music of Glenn Miller and Jimmy Dorsey. We loved country music, too, listening to shows such as Louisiana Hayride and comedies like Amos and Andy. But amidst the entertainment was, of course, the news from overseas – turmoil in China, war in Ethiopia, Hitler rising in Germany and civil war in Spain.

When the days cooled down and winter in Texas brought us indoors, we made up games to play. We also loved to draw, and my brother, Guy, was a very talented artist. John Crawford said that Guy "could draw a dog that looked like he would bark at you." Guy was both sensitive and intelligent, and I really looked up to him.

Guy always believed that the war raging through the rest of the world was going to catch up with us, some day. And if it did, he planned to do his part. In fact, he was so determined not to be left behind that he dropped out of his studies at the Unversity of Texas, even before the war, to join up. He enlisted in the Army Air Corps in April of 1941 reporting to Fort Sam Houston to begin his basic training. By the end of 1941, Guy had completed flight school and was assigned to the 35th Pursuit Squadron, based at Paine Field, Washington.

I was very proud of Guy and told everyone who would listen that my brother had won his wings and was an Army Air Corps pilot.

Like all others my age, I loved movies, but there was no theater in Zavalla, so when I wanted to see one I would have to hitchhike to Lufkin, which was twenty-five miles away. Hitchhiking was a common occurrence in those days, and because our area was so sparsely populated, I often got rides with the same people. I was particularly partial to the Saturday Matinee Tom Mix Westerns.

Before the main feature, the theaters would show newsreels. Sometimes my friends and I would talk about the newsreel scenes from Europe and Asia. We could feel the danger looming and every one of us made plans to join the service as soon as we were old enough. Guy wasn't the only one of our crowd to have joined. John's older brother, Boyd, had already enlisted in the Marine Corps and was stationed overseas in the Philippines.

The only thing that stopped me from enlisting right out of high school, was the fact that I had been given a basketball scholarship to Lon Morris College in Jacksonville, Texas. I was a good basketball player and saw this as an opportunity to play basketball while continuing my education.

It was Sunday, just after lunch, and a friend and I were walking from the cafeteria back to the Lon Morris athletic dormitory. Billy was fired up about an upcoming game with Kilgore College. Kilgore had the best record in the conference, but he was convinced that we would beat them.

"I mean come on, how can we lose?" Billy asked.

"How can we lose? Because Kilgore's got a great team," I replied. "That's how we can lose."

"But think about it," Billy said, his enthusiasm unwavering. "Eddie can beat their center at the jump, I'll get the tip off, you break to the basket, I'll pass to you and you'll make the lay up."

Billy Pearson was from Corrigon, Texas and we had played against each other all through high school. We were fierce competitors then, but now we were both playing for the Lon Morris Bearcats. Billy was a guard; I was a forward.

"It'll take more than one basket to beat them," I said.

It was Sunday, December 7th, 1941. We had gone to chapel that morning, a requirement since this was a Methodist school. Then, after chapel, we had lunch. I remember that lunch as if it were yesterday. We had baked ham, macaroni and cheese, and green peas. We had angel food cake and canned peaches for desert.

"We'll make more than one basket," Billy insisted. "Heck, I'll bet we could just do the same thing over and over again."

"Well, uh, don't you think they'll be out there trying to stop us?"

"They'll try," Billy said. "But they won't succeed. We're unstoppable, we're invincible, we're the best." By now we were in the dorm, and there was a trash can sitting just outside the door of one of the rooms. "There!" Billy said, pointing toward the trash can. "I've got the tip, break for the basket!"

I ran to the trash can, Billy threw a wadded piece of paper he was carrying, and I put it in the can.

"There, see! Two points!" Billy said enthusiastically. He made the sound of a crowd cheering. "See how easy that was?"

"Yeah, well, there were no Kilgore players trying to stop me."

"What are you going to do this afternoon?" Billy asked.

"I've got a paper to write," I said. "I thought I'd write it and listen to Sammy Kaye."

"I don't have a radio. Can I come in and listen too?"

"Sure, as long as you don't bother me while I'm writing," I said.

Going into my dorm room, I turned on the radio, then sat at my desk and pulled out some paper to start working on my assignment. Billy stretched out on my bed to listen to the radio, and after station identification, we heard the opening strains from the band of Sammy Kaye.

"From Radio City in New York, it is the pleasure of the National Broadcasting Company to bring you Sammy Kaye's Sunday Serenade, featuring his world-famed swing and sway music."

Angel In The Cockpit

After the announcer's introduction, Sammy Kaye came to the microphone.

"This is yours truly, Sammy Kaye, welcoming you most kindly to our . . .Sunday Serenade."

Following Sammy Kaye's welcome, the band vocalist, Tommy Ryan, began singing. Knowing the lyrics, Billy began singing along with him.

"This is no laughing matter . . . "

Suddenly the radio broadcast was interrupted.

"From the NBC Newsroom in New York. President Roosevelt said in a statement today that the Japanese have attacked Pearl Harbor, in Hawaii, from the air. I'll repeat that. President Roosevelt says that the Japanese have attacked Pearl Harbor, in Hawaii, from the air. This bulletin came to you from the NBC Newsroom in New York."

"What is this?" Billy asked. "Get back to the music."

I put my pen down and turned to look at the radio.

"What's a Pearl Harbor?" Billy asked.

"It's a big American Naval Base in the Pacific," I said.

The broadcast continued with Robert Trout giving his analysis of the situation.

"The details are not yet available. They will be in a few minutes. The White House is now giving out a statement. The attack was apparently made on all naval and military facilities on the principle island of Oahu. The President's brief statement was read to reporters by Stephen Early, the President's secretary. The Japanese attack on Pear Harbor would naturally mean war. Such an attack would naturally bring a counter-attack, and hostilities of this kind would mean that the President would ask Congress for a Declaration of War. There is no doubt that Congress will grant the President's request."

From the look on Billy's face, I knew that he still wasn't grasping its importance. "Does this mean like a real war? What is going on over in Europe?" he asked.

I nodded. "Yes. That's exactly what it means."

"Wow," Billy said, finally comprehending. "Wow, this is something, isn't it? I mean, this is really something."

The next day classes were suspended as the entire school gathered around radios to listen to President Roosevelt's address to the joint session of Congress. I believe it was the most dramatic speech in American History.

"Mr. Vice President, Mr. Speaker, Senators, Members of the House of Representatives: Yesterday, December 7th, 1941, a date which will live in infamy, the United States was suddenly and deliberately attacked by Naval and Air Forces of the Empire of Japan.

"The United States was at peace with that nation and at the solicitation of Japan and its empire was looking toward the maintenance of peace in the Pacific. Indeed, one hour after Japanese Air Forces had commenced bombing on the Island of Oahu, the Japanese Ambassador to the United States and his colleague delivered to the United States a formal reply to a recent American message. And while this reply stated that it seemed useless to continue the negotiations, it contained no threat nor hint of an armed attack.

"It will be recorded that the distance of Hawaii from Japan makes it obvious that the attack was planned many days or even weeks ago. During the intervening time the Japanese government has deliberately sought to deceive the United States by false statements of hope for continued peace. The attack upon the Hawaiian Islands has caused severe damage to American

and Government forces. I regret to tell you that many American lives have been lost.

"American ships, between San Francisco and Honolulu, have been torpedoed. Yesterday, the Japanese government forces attacked Malaya. Last night, Japanese forces attacked Hong Kong. Last night, Japanese Forces attacked Guam. Last night, Japanese forces attacked the Philippine Islands. Last night, Japanese forces attacked Wake Island, and this morning Japanese forces attacked Midway. Japan has therefore undertaken a surprise offensive throughout the entire Pacific area.

"No matter how long it may take us, the United States in their righteous might, will see this through to victory. With confidence in our armed forces, with the unbound determination of our people, we will gain the inevitable triumph, so help us God."

Chapter Two

Winning My Wings

One week earlier the most important thing on the mind of everyone in the athletic dormitory was the Bearcats' basketball season. Now, all we talked about, all I could think about, was the cowardly attack against us at Pearl Harbor. And, like every red-blooded American boy, I was giving some serious thought to joining the armed forces.

Although my parents wanted me to stay in school, I was chomping at the bit to join, pointing out that my brother, Guy, was already in the war. Of course my mother used that same bit of logic to try and talk me out of it. "One of my sons is at war already," she said. "Isn't that enough?"

In the chaos following the Pearl Harbor attack, Guy's squadron was assigned to fly anti-submarine patrols off the Pacific coast. But those patrols ceased on January 21, 1942, and the Squadron began a frenzied effort to pack and move to San Francisco, where they would join the forces being rushed to the defense of Australia.

They sailed on the last day of January in a converted freighter and arrived in Brisbane on February 25th. Within a month they moved to Melbourne where they mated up with their new aircraft. The planes were P-400's, an export version of the Bell P-39's the squadron had flown in the United States. The airplanes had originally been intended for the Philippines, but were diverted at sea due to the Japanese invasion.

After shaking down their new aircraft, Guy's squadron moved north to Townville and then to the defense of the beleaguered Port Moresby in New Guinea. I was intensely proud of Guy, but I envied him as well.

One April afternoon I was studying for a World History exam, though my mind wasn't in it. What did I care about the fall of Constantinople? There were greater and more important battles being fought right now. I couldn't keep my mind on the words on the page, so I kept looking through my window at the flowering dogwood and redbud trees. It was a beautiful, soft, spring day, the kind of East Texas day I would reflect upon many times over the next sixty years of my life.

Someone knocked on my door and, thinking it was Billy, I called out to him.

"Come in and no, you can't copy my homework. Do your own."

The door opened slightly. "Ray?"

It wasn't Billy's voice. It was the voice of our School Chaplain.

"Reverend Owen," I said, standing quickly. "Come in, come in." I hurried over to open the door for him.

Although our chaplain was a basketball fan and would from time to time visit us to talk about basketball, the season was over. Besides, the expression on his face was very strained.

"Is something wrong?" I asked.

"Ray, I just, uh, spoke to the dean." Reverend Owen started.

"You spoke to the dean about me? What about?"

"The dean got a phone call," Reverend Owen said.

Angel In The Cockpit

I didn't know where he was going with this, but I was sure I wasn't going to like it.

Reverend Owen ran his hand through his hair, then put it on my shoulder. "I hate to tell you this, son. But the phone call was about your brother, Guy. He has been reported missing."

"Missing?" I asked. I wasn't entirely familiar with the term. What did he mean, missing? "What are you talking about? Guy wouldn't run away from anything. What do you mean he is missing?" My response was angry and defensive.

Reverend Owen looked shocked at my reaction, then he realized what I was saying, and he shook his head. "No, no, I don't mean that," he said, shaking his head. "Missing is a term the military uses when they haven't found the body."

"The body?"

"Ray, your brother was shot down by the Japanese. His plane went down and nobody reported seeing a parachute. He is presumed killed."

The chaplain's words hit me like a baseball bat in the stomach. I took several steps back, then sat in my chair, staring at him.

"I'm sorry, son," the chaplain said. "I can't tell you how sorry I am."

I didn't answer.

"If you would allow me, Ray, I'd like to pray with you now."

I nodded, and bowed my head, but I didn't hear a word of the chaplain's prayer. I thought of Guy, of him teaching me how to shoot a rifle, how to bait a hook, how to swim, and how to ride a bicycle. I could see him bent over a piece of paper drawing a picture, and I could see the smile on his face as he teased me about being the "baby" of the family.

"I'll talk to the dean," the chaplain said. "I'm sure you'll want to be with your parents for a few days. I'll see to it that you are excused from your classes."

"Thanks," I said.

Within minutes, the other guys in the dorm heard of my loss and they came into my room, singly, and in pairs, to offer their condolences. I'm sure they had words of comfort for me, but I don't think I even noticed them. I couldn't get around the grief over the loss of my brother.

When I got back home to Zavalla, there was no funeral for Guy, because we had no one to bury. But our church did hold a memorial service, which was just like a funeral, though without the interment. Then, sadly, even as we were planning the memorial service for Guy, I learned that Boyd, the older brother of my best friend, John, had been taken prisoner by the Japanese when the Philippines fell.

Later that day, after we returned home from Guy's memorial service, I told my parents what I had been thinking about for a long time.

"I'm not going back to school," I said. "I'm joining the Navy."

"Oh, Ray, no," my mother said. "Please." She began crying. "I don't think I could live through losing another of my sons."

"I have to, Mama," I said. "Don't you see? I have to."

"I . . . I won't allow it," she said, resolutely.

"Gilley," my dad said. "He has to."

"Thanks, Dad," I said, surprised, but very grateful that he understood.

"Be careful, boy," he said.

"I will be," I promised. I was just mouthing the response. Being careful was not one of my priorities.

I joined the Navy's V-S Aviation Pilots Program on April 29, 1942. I reported to Naval Air Station, Dallas, with a group of about twenty volunteers from the Texas-Oklahoma area. We were joined by an equal number of recruits from the Detroit, Michigan, area and began our basic training in June of 1942.

As we moved through training for the next few months, the Civil War was revisited many times by the group. This was always done in a friendly way however, since it was very clear that the "Yankees" and the "Rebels" there, were of one mind and spirit – to avenge the attack on their county by the Japanese.

Our basic training started when we were greeted by our drill instructor, a Marine Sergeant named Agro. We never knew his first name. In fact, when one of the cadets asked him what his first name was he replied, very sternly, "Cadet, to you my first name is Sergeant. Do you understand that?"

"Yes Sergeant," he replied.

"Do all of you understand that?" he shouted.

"*Yes Sergeant!*" we shouted back.

Later, as we faced the strenuous training and the stress of combat, it became clear to each of us that the rigorous discipline Sergeant Agro put us through was for our own good.

In basic training they taught us to fly, but it almost seemed to take a back seat to the six to eight hours of ground school we endured every day. The ground school curriculum included celestial navigation, dead reckoning, aerodynamics, Morse code, semaphore, blinker, radio and recognition.

To give an example of the detail we had to go into in all of these subjects, I'll use recognition. We were required to be able to recognize every ship and aircraft of the Japanese and American forces. In the final quiz we were shown a half-second flash of a silhouette of different ships and aircraft; then we had to identify each one. This may seem a stringent requirement, but you certainly did not want to shoot down one of your own aircraft in a dogfight or bomb one of your own ships. Later, with the split second decisions of combat, we learned that this training served us well.

Basic flight training went smoothly, but the first 10 hours of flight were the hardest. It was during this time that our instructor attempted to teach us everything we needed to know about flight before he would allow us to take a plane up solo.

I particularly remember one flight. My instructor was teaching me the art of 'slips to a circle.' This technique was taught to allow you to 'slip' the aircraft - to slow it down so you could land on a small field - a vital skill for landing on aircraft carriers. The maneuver requires you to cut the power, pull back on the stick and put your left wing down as you turn toward the circle, while at the same time feeding in opposite rudder. You hold this slip attitude until you approach the circle; then you level the plane out just before touch down.

On one such flight, I shot several circles and was doing fairly well in hitting the target. The instructor said, "OK Hawkins, shoot one more and if you hit the circle you get an 'up check.'" I made my approach and as I neared the circle I could see I was a little high and was going to overshoot. I eased back on the stick, and at about twenty feet over the circle, the plane stalled, falling directly into the center of the target. I added power, gained altitude and returned to the air base. The instructor was livid.

"Hawkins it's a good thing I told you if you hit the circle I would give you an 'up check', because for that bit of flying you would certainly get a 'down'." He sighed. "However, you did hit the circle, which is what I ask of you, so I am going to give you a shaky 'up.'"

After fifty-three basic training flights, totaling 68 hours in the air, and many more hours of ground school, we were shipped off to the Naval Air Station, Corpus Christi, Texas, for intermediate training.

In intermediate training, they taught us to fly at night on instruments and by radio navigation. Most of us thought we were wasting our time. We wanted to be learning how to shoot, bomb, strafe and get into combat as soon as we could. But wiser heads prevailed, as they convinced us that this part of flying was just as important as the pure combat phase.

Upon completion of intermediate training we made fifty-six more flights, equaling another sixty-eight hours in the air, plus much more ground school. Following that, we were transferred to Naval Air Station, Kingsville, Texas for the next phase of our training.

This was our advanced training, and here we did learn how to use our guns, shooting at targets in the air and at targets on the ground. We learned the art of glide bombing and the use of the basic fighter unit known as a division. A division was made up of two sections of two planes each. Flying in this formation, we were taught how to attack the enemy, while at the same time protecting each other. Additional night flying was also on the curriculum, and after eighty-five hours of intense training in the air, we completed the advanced syllabus. On 1 January 1943, we were commissioned ensigns in the Navy and received our gold wings, designating us as naval aviators.

Emotions ran high among those of us who finished the program. We had read and listened to all of the war news. We had poured over every scrap of information we could find on the carrier battles of the Coral Sea and Midway. We were heartened when the United States struck back with Doolittle's Raid and at Guadalcanal. We followed the news of the savage naval engagements in the Solomon Islands. And we awaited our orders that would send us to our squadrons, bringing us one step closer to entering combat. The orders would also designate the type of flying each of us would be doing. Some would go to fighter squadrons, others to either dive bombing or torpedo squadrons, while some would be assigned to transport aircraft.

The New Ensign

I was elated to be assigned to Fighter Squadron 31 (VF-31) that was forming at Naval Air Station, Atlantic City, New Jersey. As a fighter pilot I knew my chances would be better to fulfill my vow to avenge my brother's death at the hands of the Japanese.

Before joining my squadron, there were two more bits of training I had to complete. I was ordered to Naval Air Station, Miami, Florida, for operational training which consisted of being checked out in an actual combat aircraft Since I was ordered to a fighter squadron, I flew the F2A Brewster Buffalo.

The F2A Brewster Buffalo, was originally in direct competition with the Grumman Wildcat, actually winning the Navy contract for the first carrier-based monoplane fighter in 1938. Production problems delayed its introduction until late 1939. By that time, vastly improved Wildcats were entering Navy service. An engine upgrade brought some improvement, but not enough. In service against the Japanese during the first six months of the war, it was found to be slow, lacking in agility, under-gunned and a maintenance burden. The Buffaloes were removed from combat service in June of 1942 and relegated to use as a trainer until 1944, when they were finally withdrawn from service altogether.

In the Buffalo we did air-to-air gunnery and strafing with two 50-caliber guns that fired through the turning propeller. We also did live bomb drops using 100-pound bombs. There was also some individual training in air to air combat by instructors who had survived combat against Japanese Zeros. With operational training completed successfully, there was one more important requirement - becoming qualified to land and operate from the deck of an aircraft carrier.

I received this training at Naval Air Station, Norfolk, Virginia. The aircraft carrier, *USS Charger,* was operating outside Chesapeake Bay for landing qualifications. This requirement for a naval aviator is often likened to the saying, "Not only do I have to find a postage stamp in a vast ocean, after I find it I have to land on it." Certainly this is overstated but it does require a bit of finesse. There were many that did not meet the requirement and were assigned something other than carrier aviation.

The **USS Charger** began her life as the cargo/passenger ship **Rio de la Plata**. The ship was acquired by the Navy in spring of 1941 and converted to an aircraft carrier at Newport News Shipbuilding and Drydock Co. She entered service with the Royal Navy as the training carrier, **HMS Charger**, but was shortly returned to the US Navy. The *Charger* served as a training carrier throughout the war and was eventually reconverted to merchant service in 1949, as the **Fairsea**.

After making my required twelve carrier landings on the Charger, I reported to VF-31 at the Naval Air Station Atlantic City, New Jersey, on 13 April 1943. It was hard to believe that I had gained the expertise required of a fledgling naval aviator in a short ten months of intensive training. With that training, I was about to join a fighting unit, to enter combat flying from the deck of an aircraft carrier, and to become part of the most massive combat fleet ever assembled

Things began to pick up when five of us received orders to go to the Grumman plant to pick up airplanes for the squadron. There had been a lot of scuttlebutt that we would be flying the old battle tested F4F Wildcat. We were elated to learn we would be picking up the new F6F Hellcat. This airplane had been designed to compete more evenly with the Japanese Zero and served the Navy as its carrier-based fighter for the duration of the war. The Navy had ordered maximum production of the Hellcat. The five of us had never seen an F6F before and we were awed by its size in comparison to the familiar Wildcat. We received a thorough checkout on the Hellcat from the Grumman test pilots. Then we manned our birds, took off and headed for Atlantic City. The runway that was supposed to be finished to receive us was fouled, so we had to land at a small airport in nearby Plesantville, New Jersey. The planes remained at Plesantville until the Air Station was ready to receive them. It gave all of the pilots a moral boost. Plesantville was only a short distance from the Air Station and we all could get over to admire the new planes and start checkout.

> The primary carrier-based fighter for the US Navy at the start of WWII was the Grumman **F4F Wildcat**. The Wildcat was a rugged fighter with great ability to absorb damage and stay in the air. It immediately encountered the **Mitsubishi A6M3 Zero-sen Zero**. The Zero was faster and far more maneuverable than the Wildcat with a tighter turning radius and a much greater rate of climb. Anticipating trouble from the Zero, the Navy issued a specification for an improved carrier-based fighter before the war even began. The **Grumman F6F Hellcat** was the answer. The Hellcat retained its predecessor's ability to absorb punishment, and added speed and maneuverability to match the Zero. Entering service in late 1943, it remained the Navy's favored fighter through the remainder of the war.

The squadron and air group slowly began to take shape as officers and enlisted men continued to report in. Squadron organization was established and a course of training put together. What we didn't have in experience, we made up for in enthusiasm. We had every confidence that we would get it done. We did have a few combat veterans, but the bulk of the thirty-two fighter pilots were ensigns, fresh from training.

Our squadron training began in earnest in the middle of May. We lost three pilots in training crashes, had a few forced landings, two cases of wheels folding on takeoff and other minor snafus. I had seen death during my training, but now it was closer to everyone in our squadron, and it nearly happened to me, long before I saw my first Japanese plane.

You have to realize that by this time all of us "Young Tigers" were feeling our oats. Here we were, flying the Navy's newest fighter planes and getting the feeling we were hot stuff. One day I decided to see how high I could get one of the Hellcats to go. As I leveled at 25,000 feet I began getting light headed and dizzy; then I realized that I was undergoing the first symptoms of oxygen deprivation. I knew I had to get down fast before I passed out and crashed. I flipped the Hellcat over, pulled through into a Split-S, and headed for the ground.

I watched the altimeter winding down, and the airspeed winding up. I was doing better than four-hundred-fifty miles per hour! It was an exhilarating feeling, this feeling of speed, and I knew at the time that there were probably very few people in the world who had ever gone this fast. I pulled back on the stick, preparing for the G-force I would experience from such a pull out.

But to my surprise, nothing happened! The airplane continued plummeting toward the ground.

"What is this?" I asked aloud. I pulled the stick back farther, but still there was no reaction.

This can't be right! At this speed I should have had an almost instantaneous response! In fact, I knew to keep my control movement limited so as not to put too much force on the airframe.

The speed continued to climb, five-hundred miles per hour. The altimeter continued to wind down, and now read three-thousand feet. I was almost totally nose down, and I watched as a tree below me grew larger and larger. I could see the individual leaves on that tree!

"Try the rudder, Ray."

The voice was as clear as if it were my instructor talking into my headset. *But it was Guys' voice!*

I chopped the throttle and cycled the rudders back and forth causing the plane to fishtail. When I did, the elevator grabbed hold and the airplane came out of its screaming dive. G-forces pressed me back in the seat and just before I had a momentary blackout, I saw that I had descended to no more than fifteen-hundred feet. I was still in excess of four-hundred miles per hour as I started climbing again. I pushed the stick forward and got a second or two of total weightlessness, experiencing the same sensation our astronauts would experience many years later, when they made similar parabolic flights in the "Vomit Comet." Finally, I got the airplane in a straight and level flight and I brought it back home, an older, and much wiser pilot. It only takes one of these harrowing flights to make a hot pilot simmer down to a smarter pilot.

What I had not realized before that maneuver was that when the Hellcat reached an excessive speed in a steep dive, it's large round nose section would create a vacuum effect around the tail surfaces of the aircraft. This vacuum effect made it almost impossible to recover from the dive.

"Thanks, God," I breathed in prayer, "and thanks for sending Guy to help out."

It was funny, because although I knew it was impossible to have actually heard Guy's voice, I was convinced that I had. I knew then that Guy was with me, an angel in my cockpit.

Once we began checking out in the Hellcat, we learned to appreciate its power and maneuverability. Our confidence in the plane was well justified, because of the 6,477 Japanese planes shot down by carrier-based aircraft during WWII, the Hellcat accounted for 4,947.

Chapter Three

My First Kill

The intensive training lasted for about three months before the squadron was ordered to Norfolk, Virginia, to go aboard the *USS Cabot* (CVL-28). The *Cabot* was a new aircraft carrier constructed by the New York Shipbuilding Corp. at Hampton, New Jersey. The air group reported aboard and the ship got underway in September for a shakedown and Operational Readiness Inspection at, and around, Trinidad. The shakedown began with a sorrowful note when one of our fighter pilots was killed making an approach and landing on the ship. Operations by the air group on the *Cabot* became routine and the ship and squadrons began to meld together. After a month of continuous operations, the ship returned to the States with a crew and an air group who were happy with their accomplishments.

The *Cabot* moored at the Philadelphia Navy Shipyard for some very minor repairs and authorized leave to as many of the crew as could be spared. The air group Commander gave a five-day leave to all hands and directed us to report to Naval Air Station, Quonset Point, Rhode Island, prepared for embarkation. Everyone was elated. This was it. Finally the training became a memory, and we would be heading west for our first test of combat.

USS Cabot (CVL-28) – The *Cabot* was an *Independence* class light carrier, born out of wartime necessity. As the threat of war loomed in the spring of 1941, the U.S. Navy faced a problem – they needed carriers in a hurry and the large fleet carriers were expensive and took years to build. The Navy came up with a program to build smaller, cheaper carriers. Light cruisers currently under construction were converted to light carriers. The *Cabot* was built in just ten months and Launched on April 4, 1942. Although it lacked the aircraft capacity of its larger sisters (32 vs. 96 planes), as well as being lightly armed and armored, the *Independence* class served well throughout the war.

With good-byes said to families, friends and loved ones, on November 7, 1943, with the air group aboard, the *Cabot* weighed anchor and set sail for the combat zone. As the ship headed for the Panama Canal, there was only time for some very light flight operations. This available spare time gave the pilots a chance to ponder their entry into combat and the dangers of the job ahead.

After the ship had passed through the canal, we headed north for San Diego where we made a one night scheduled stop to take on passengers for transport to Hawaii. The following morning the *Cabot* departed for Pearl Harbor. The ship was traveling alone, so it was scheduled for a high-speed transit to thwart any enemy submarines that might be lurking along the route. On 27 November 1943, the *Cabot* was moored at Ford Island, Hawaii, and the air group flew off the ship to Kaneohe Naval Air Station on Oahu. Many hours of refresher training were done on targets located around the islands, and while conducting flight operations from the *Cabot* at sea.

Angel In The Cockpit

The *Cabot* (CVL-28) joined the 5th Fleet at the very end of 1943. She was assigned to Task Force 58 (the carrier groups) and Task Group 58.2. TG 58.2 consisted of the *Essex* class carriers *Bunker Hill* (CV-17) and *Wasp* (CV-18), along with another light carrier the *Monterey* (CVL-26).

The fleet, of which I was now a part, put to sea on January 15, 1944, in preparation for the landings in the Marshall Islands. During the sortie the *Cabot* crossed the equator and the international date line at the same time. For this the crew qualified as "Shellbacks". We were initiated by the "Old Salts" and admitted to the order of the "Golden Dragons." Morale ran high, and we were eager to put our skill against the enemy.

These desires were fulfilled on the morning January 29th when a full-scale attack was launched against the island of Roi in the Marshall group. Our mission was to gain control of the air space around the landing sites and to protect the fleet from attack.

Other than the combat air patrols, there were the "call" missions which we flew in direct support of the Marines making amphibious landings. We would report in to a ground controller, then loiter in place until we were called for strikes on targets that were giving the troops trouble. These targets would be designated on a grid map carried by each pilot. The ground controller might say, "Hit enemy rolling equipment in southwest corner of sector H unit 6." The pilot located the target and attacked it by strafing with his six .50 caliber guns or releasing any bombs he had on board.

In this type of operation, the antiaircraft fire is always heavy, with a lot of small arms fire being expected, because of the low altitude. To counteract this fire the pilot is constantly changing altitude, speed and direction to keep the gunners from zeroing in on him.

It was on one such mission that I experienced my first harrowing combat flight. The controller had assigned a machine gun emplacement as my target. I located it on my grid map and positioned myself for the attack. In my dive, I received antiaircraft fire from both sides, and I could see the two men in the machine gun nest trying to raise their gun to return my fire.

I obliterated the gun emplacement before it could return fire. As I made my escape run, I pulled up sharply and entered a cloud at about 2,000 feet. I thought the overcast was no more than a few thousand feet thick, so I held my climb thinking I would break out, recover and report back in to my ground controller. As I continued my climb through the clouds, though, the air became very turbulent and I fell off into a spin. I broke out of the clouds at about 2,000 feet, heading straight down. I had memories of my high speed dive back in the States when I was just transitioning into the Hellcat.

I managed to recover from the spin, but I wound up at about 200 feet over the machine gun nest I had just attacked. Luckily, the nest was out of action and I guess the other gunners did not expect me back so soon. I regained altitude, then contacted my ground controller and resumed my station awaiting another assignment.

On one such mission, while loitering, I watched the big guns of our ships pounding the beach. It was a box seat for a fascinating show. When the battleships would let go a salvo from their sixteen-inch guns, you could follow the shells all the way to their target, then actually see the shockwaves formed by the instant condensation of the air around the point of impact.

Then I saw something that sickened me. One of our own shells hit a dive-bomber that was orbiting over the beach. The plane disintegrated and the shell continued on to its target.

With the Marines safely ashore in the Marshall Islands, we continued our operations against the heavily fortified Japanese base on Truk. This atoll, along with the rest of the Caroline Islands, had been placed under Japanese mandate at the end of World War I.

The Japanese used that time to great advantage. They built five airfields around the deep natural harbor of the lagoon and turned Truk into a major naval base. At its zenith, Truk held five-hundred aircraft and provided anchorage and support facilities for a significant portion of the Japanese fleet. The base was vital to the Japanese wave of conquest that swept through the Pacific at the start of the war, and it was our mission to neutralize it.

The mission, called "Operation Hailstone", was to destroy any units of the Japanese fleet anchored at Truk and to render the airfields and support facilities unusable so that our forces in the Marshalls could be safe from attack.

On one of our missions the bombers of our air group sent an 8,000 ton supply ship to its grave, and we caught thirteen twin-engine Japanese "Betty" bombers on the runway of the airfield and left them in flames.

> The "Betty" was officially the Mitsubishi G4M medium bomber. It could carry more than a ton of bombs and deliver them to targets more than twenty-five hundred miles away. Its great range made it the workhorse of Japanese aviation throughout the war. In battle, it suffered from light armament, no armor for the pilot and a lack of self-sealing fuel tanks. These factors limited its combat survivability.

During my three combat strikes in this operation, I was a member of a flight of six aircraft armed with 1,000-pound, armor-piercing bombs. Our mission was to drop a spread of bombs down the runway of an enemy airfield. Each bomb had a time-sensitive and motion-sensitive fuse. The bomb would explode if anyone tried to remove it, or if unmolested, it would go off when the timer expired. The six bombs were set to explode at varying intervals over a span of several days. The bomb I was carrying was fused for twelve hours after impact. This period would keep the airfield unusable for some time and guarantee that sleep would be at a premium for the occupants of Truk.

As Task Force 58 retired from Truk, we all left with a feeling of increased confidence that we could meet and beat the Japanese on all fronts. We had struck one of their most heavily fortified military bases and left it in shambles. We established air superiority over the island, destroyed two-hundred-fifty aircraft in the air and on the ground, and left our time-sensitive thousand pound calling cards spread about the airfields. We sank fifteen warships and sent one hundred thirty-seven thousand tons of merchant shipping to the bottom of the lagoon. air group 31 had accomplished all of our assigned missions without the loss of a pilot or aircraft. The success of the Truk Operation was particularly satisfying to members of Task Fore 58, as it felt like a partial repayment for the attack on Pearl Harbor. I had taken part in all of this, but I still had not seen a Japanese airplane in the air, and I was anxious to try my dog fighting skills.

Task Group 58.2 suffered one bit of damage when the *USS Intrepid* took a torpedo hit on her starboard side. The <u>Cabot</u>, the cruisers, *San Francisco* and *Wichita,* plus four destroyers were formed into Task Unit 58.24 to escort the *Intrepid* back to Kwajalein for repairs. After we finished beating up Truk, Task Force 58 turned its attention west to the island of Palau. We were tasked with the destruction of the military installations there in support of the planned occupation of Hollandia in New Guinea, and we rejoined the fleet in time for the operation.

Angel In The Cockpit

Our strikes on Palau began on 30 March 1944, and lasted two days. On the first day of attacks, four planes from our fighter squadron encountered nine Japanese "Jill" torpedo planes on the way to attack the force. A major dogfight broke out, and the nine enemy aircraft were sent down in flames. Our torpedo planes sank a 7000-ton seaplane tender, attacked a Japanese light cruiser, forcing it to beach itself to escape sinking. It was on this strike that our air group suffered its first combat casualty when one of our torpedo bombers and its crew of three failed to return. More than forty-five years later, this aircraft was found in the jungle growth of Palau with the remains of the crew still in the aircraft.

After two days of air attacks, Task Force 58 had sunk three destroyers, seventeen freighters, five oilers, and damaged seventeen other ships. Our aircraft had also bombed the airfields, and mined the waters around Palau to immobilize enemy shipping.

I was still without an air-to-air victory.

With the military capability of the Palau Islands wrecked, Task Force 58 steamed southeast at full speed to arrive off Woleai Island on 1 April. Massive strikes were launched against the military bases on Woleai and met with little resistance except for a smattering of antiaircraft fire. An aircraft from another carrier was shot down in the harbor, and two of our fighters were assigned escort for a small seaplane from one of the cruisers that was attempting a rescue. Our planes kept the shore batteries busy while the seaplane landed in the water and retrieved the pilot.

We received one scare when it was reported that twelve "Betty" bombers were inbound to attack the force. As it turned out, the report was false. There weren't twelve Betty bombers, there was only one, lone reconnaissance plane. My friend, Frank

Hayde, shot it down. Frank was the first of the four of us in the sixth division, to get a kill.

That evening, the four of us in the division, Stewart, me, Loomis, and Frank, gathered around to watch the squadron artist paint a tiny Japanese flag on the side of Frank's plane, just under the canopy. We toasted him with coffee, the strongest beverage authorized on the ship.

Frank and I used to have some bodacious conversations, late in the night. We would argue about things that made absolutely no sense, such as whether a fly took off forward or backward, or whether or not a fish actually drank water. Once, we even got into an argument as to whether Santa Claus carried a red bag or a brown bag. Now, bear in mind, that neither of us had believed in Santa Claus for many, many years, but that didn't stop the intensity of the argument.

Of course, we also talked about home, and about our families. Frank knew about Guy being killed early in the war. He also was the only person I had ever told that sometimes, I felt that Guy was in the cockpit with me.

"If you think he's there, he's there," Guy said. "I've always had the belief that when you think of someone who has died, it's the same as if they are there."

If you are going to be in a war, a long way from home, family, and friends that you grew up with, it was good to have a friend like Frank.

With the military installations of Palau and Woleai Islands neutralized and no longer a threat to the amphibious assault on Hollandia, Task Force 58 retired to the Majuro Lagoon. After taking on supplies and ammunition, we got underway once more on 13 April for the scheduled 21 April invasion of Hollandia.

Angel In The Cockpit

As Task Force 58 approached the target, air strikes were launched and shore bombardment began against Hollandia and the island of Wake. On "D" Day the ground assault began as a swarm of landing craft headed toward the beach. This was the largest amphibious operation yet in the Southwest Pacific. Task Force 58 had more than 200 ships including carriers, battleships, cruisers, and destroyers assigned just to cover the landings.

With the invasion going well, the air strikes and the shore bombardment continued. The troops were firmly on the beach and fortifying their position. Japanese resistance came mostly from a few heavily dug in troops who were determined to hold out till death. Our air group's last strikes in support of the operation were launched against Wadke and Sawar Islands to ensure that no resistance would come from Japanese installations there. We left Wadke and Sawar Islands in flames.

Task Group 58.2 was ordered to detach from the rest of Task Force 58 and proceed to Truk where it would launch a second series of attacks on the atoll. Our mission was to render Truk incapable of launching any air or surface raids against Hollandia.

In the two-day operation at Truk, we bombed and strafed buildings, hangers, barracks and fuel dumps on Eaten Island, leaving the airfield in smoke and flames. The military installations on Dublon Island, including the seaplane base, received the same treatment.

The resistance put up by the Japanese during this second raid on Truk proved somewhat greater than on the first raid. Japanese scout planes spotted the task force on its approach, and this time we did not have the luxury of surprise. The Japanese launched a torpedo attack against us.

This was on the 29th of April, and it was on this, my twenty-fifth mission that I finally got my first kill.

And this brings me back to where I started this story, sitting in the cockpit of my Hellcat at 0545 on the morning of the 29th of April, 1944, waiting to launch.

Dramatically, the launch officer squatted, faced the front of the carrier and pointed toward the end of the deck. The catapult was fired and the Hellcat hurled down the flight deck, moving so fast that all around me was a blur.

The deck fell away and I was over the water. Clearing the bow, I turned to the right. As I did so, I was shocked to see right in front of me and perfectly lined up in my gun sights, one of the approaching Japanese torpedo bombers. With my adrenalin pumping, I pulled the trigger and felt the shake as my six machine guns began firing. Bright bits of light streamed quickly before me and converged on the torpedo bomber. The heavy concentration of .50 caliber shells tore the enemy plane to pieces and sent him flaming into the water.

"Good show, Hawk!" someone said. I recognized my friend Frank Hayde's voice.

"Keep the radio clear." That was Stewart's voice.

Even as I was shooting down my first kill, and the rest of my division was taking off behind me, the entire flight of Japanese torpedo bombers was upon our fleet. The ships of our formation opened up on them with antiaircraft fire. All around me I could see streaking balls of light, each ball of light an anti-aircraft shell. Between each ball of light, I knew were four more, unseen, shells, just as deadly. Puffs of ugly black smoke filled the sky and large geysers of water shot up into the air, caused by the five-inch shells hitting the sea around the low flying aircraft.

To the crews on the ships the thumping pom-pom guns and bursting shells must have been deafening, but to me it was eerily quiet. You have to understand though, that when I say it was quiet, I am speaking in relative terms only. What I mean is, I could not hear the gunfire because all sound was drowned out by the scream of my own airplane engine.

Realizing quickly that I was in the direct line of fire, I maneuvered to get out of the way. I pulled up into a half loop, then rolled out on top and found myself trailing enemy aircraft through the formation.

There were twenty-six ships in the fleet with an average of fifty guns per ship, all firing at a rate of sixty rounds per minute. That was over 1,300 explosions every second, and I was flying right through the middle of it! It wasn't likely that the gunners were going to take the time to attempt to identify their targets. I was an aircraft, I was flying through the formation, I was fair game. To make matters worse, the climbing loop had bled off most of my airspeed so that by the time I rolled out on top, I was way behind the Japanese bombers, and unable to close the gap.

I know the flight through the task group couldn't have taken much more than a couple of minutes, but to me it seemed a lifetime. The antiaircraft fire lit up the sky like a Fourth of July fireworks celebration around the Washington monument. I could see the deadly streaks of tracer fire going over, under and out in front of me. My only option was to say a silent prayer and press on. To this day, I can hardly believe that I got through all that antiaircraft fire without a scratch, but I did. And although I didn't "hear the voice" of Guy this time, again I had a very strong feeling that he was in the cockpit with me.

As it turned out, I needn't have worried about our gunners. They were accurate enough to take out four of the attacking torpedo bombers. Luckily, I made it through the intense antiaircraft fire and climbed to altitude, where I was under control of our friendly fighter director.

After the Jap planes left, I landed and taxied into the position indicated by the deck crew. One of them climbed up and began unfastening my parachute and harness, even as the wings were being folded. I stepped out onto the narrow, black, reinforced portion of the wing, then hopped down from the trailing edge of the wing and onto the deck. With my helmet chin strap hanging down, and my bright yellow May West gaping open, I walked over to the carrier island and stood there for a moment. Glancing at my watch I saw that it was 0620. Barely half-an-hour had passed since the launch officer gave me the signal to go to full power!

"Alright, Hawk!" someone shouted. "You got one!"

Turning, I saw Frank Hayde coming toward me, grinning from ear to her. I smiled back at him.

"Yeah, I did, didn't I?"

"That has to be the fastest kill ever!" Frank said. Using his hands, he demonstrated me taking off then shooting down the Jap plane. "Tat, tat, tat, tat, tat," he said, mimicking the sound of the guns and he flew his hands. He opened the fingers of the hand that was the Jap plane, and showed it going down. "Splash one Jap! Damn, your gear hadn't even come up yet, had it?" he said.

I laughed. "I really don't know," he said. "It all happened so fast."

"It did that, all right," Hayde said.

By that time several of the other planes had been recovered and the pilots all came over to talk to me and to Willie Carr, who I learned, then, had also gotten one. Then a young sailor came up.

"Mr. Hawkins?"

"Yes?"

"Sir, CAG wants to see you in the CIC."

"Hey," Ensign Loomis said. "You know what this is, don't you? CAG is going to give you a medal!"

"Carr got one too. Did he ask for Carr?" I questioned the sailor.

"No, sir, he just said have Mr. Hawkins report to me on the double," the sailor said.

On the double didn't sound exactly like the way a senior officer would summon someone if he was going to give them a medal. I didn't know what this was about, but I didn't feel all that comfortable going to see him.

When I stepped into the Combat Information Center I stood just inside the door watching all the activity. Everywhere I looked there were sailors talking on the radio, manning radar screens, and plotting positions of the ships and planes by using grease pencils on a large, transparent, board. Lt. Commander Winston was standing by the board studying the layout that showed the position of the few *Cabot* airplanes that were still aloft, as well as the plotted positions of the Japanese planes that were leaving.

"Sir?" I said. "You wanted to see me?"

Winston turned, looked at me for a moment, then he sighed and shook his head. "You are the luckiest son of a bitch on earth," he said.

Smiling, I nodded. "Yes, sir. I took off and the Jap was right there in front of me. All I had to do was pull the trigger."

"No," he said. "I'm not talking about that. I'm talking about the fact that you flew through the ack-ack barrage of the entire fleet and didn't get a scratch. What were you thinking?"

"I don't know, sir," I said. "I guess I was just trying to chase the Japs away from our ship."

The expression on Winston's face softened, and he broke into a big smile, then extended his hand. "It was also some of the best flying I've ever seen. And you showed exactly the kind of aggressiveness that makes a great fighter pilot. Congratulations."

I smiled, and let out my breath in relief. I thought I was about to be reamed out, instead, I was being congratulated.

"Thank you, sir," I said.

Chapter Four

Mariannas Turkey Shoot

When speaking of the Mariannas Turkey Shoot, most historians are referring to the air battles that took place on the 19th of June 1944. The importance of that air battle cannot be overstressed, because it smashed Japanese naval aviation as a combat arm. For the remainder of the war Japanese naval air was relegated to a mere sideshow.

The successful occupation of the Gilbert Islands in November of 1943, and the Marshall Islands in February of 1944, had given the US Navy a firm foothold in the Central Pacific. The raids against Truk, Palau and Woleai were followed by the amphibious assault on Hollandia. The strategy of "island hopping" was working as planned.

Although the Japanese still had forces in the Carolines, these troops were cut off and could only receive a dribble of supplies by submarine. Land-based aircraft, from bases in the Marshalls, Gilberts and New Guinea, pounded these isolated bases regularly and maintained the blockade. Truk and Woleai were no longer threats.

In March of 1944, the Naval High Command made a pivotal decision. The massive Japanese bases in the Carolines would be neutralized by air strikes and then bypassed. Our next target would be the more thinly held islands of the Mariannas. This strategy would put our forces a thousand miles closer to the Philippines and the Japanese home islands in one daring leap.

Seizing the Mariannas would be a direct threat to the Japanese. Japan depended on the rich resources of the Indies: oil, rubber and many more essential goods, to maintain the economy of the home islands and support war production. American submarines had already wreaked havoc among the Japanese merchant shipping. Bases in the Mariannas would not only directly threaten the Philippines, but would also put the vital sea-lanes within range of our attack planes. The home islands would gradually grind to a halt without the resources of the Indies.

But the most significant aspect of the operation was to provide bases for our long-range bombers. From the Mariannas, B-29s would be able to stike cities like Tokyo, Yokohama and Nagasaki. It was, in fact, the beginning of the end for Japan.

The Japanese fleet had not been very active in 1943 and early 1944. In truth, the Japanese faced two problems. First, much of the fleet had been disbursed to bases in the Indies so that they would be closer to the sources of oil and would have sufficient fuel to operate. Second, the carrier battles of 1942 and the meat-grinder of the Solomons had taken a heavy toll on Japanese carriers and carrier pilots. The ships had been repaired and replaced, but the stock of pilots was refilling slowly. Training a carrier pilot took too long, and Japan was running out of time. Japanese naval aviators were considered a very elite group, and no provisions had been made for rapidly training large numbers to replace wartime casualties.

In the South Pacific, forces under the command of General Douglas MacArthur had blazed a bloody trail along the coast of New Guinea. Most of the Solomon Islands had been seized and the lines of communication to Australia were secure. The

Japanese base at Rabaul, on the northern tip of New Britain, had been neutralized, pounded by unceasing air raids and cut off from any hope of reinforcement by the advances of the Fifth Fleet in the Central Pacific. Even now, a massive force of airplanes and men were gathering for MacArthur's promised return to the Philippines.

First the Mariannas - then the Philippines.

The execution of this bold plan was the task of the U.S. Navy's Fifth Fleet. The major combat element of the Fifth Fleet was Task Force 58. It is a tribute to the industrial might of the United States that, while we ended 1942 with only two operational Carriers, two battleships, and a mere handful of cruisers and destroyers in the entire Pacific Ocean, by early 1944 the Fifth Fleet boasted seven large fleet carriers, eight light carriers, seven fast new battleships, and Cruisers, destroyers, and submarines by the score.

Task Force 58, the carrier component of the Fifth Fleet, was divided into four task groups, each group consisting of four carriers and four cruisers. The ships of the surface group, Task Group 58.7, were normally spread out among the carriers, adding two battleships, a cruiser and several destroyers to the available antiaircraft fire from each Task Group. There were nearly nine hundred combat aircraft aboard the carriers of the four Groups.

Flying from the deck of the *Cabot* in Task Group 58.2, we took part in Task Force 58's pre-invasion softening-up and provided direct support for the landings in the Marshall Islands. We flew air strikes against Roi, Namour and Kwajalein Islands in the Kwajalein Atoll. To ensure the safety of our troops in the Marshall Islands we struck the huge Japanese base at the Truk Atoll in the Caroline Islands, hitting the islands of Eaten, Dublon and Moen. In preparation for the amphibious assault on Hollandia, New Guinea, we hit the Palau Island group, with strikes on Anguar, Pelliellu and Babobulthuap Islands. In New Guinea we flew softening-up strikes on Hollandia, while supporting the amphibious landings. We struck Woleai, Wadke and Sawar Islands, and made another raid on Truk to ensure that the island's ability to threaten our forces had been crushed.

With the troops ashore and secure in their positions, in Hollandia, Task Force 58 withdrew to Majuro Lagoon to refit and rearm during the month of May. On 8 June 1944 we were steaming west toward the Mariannas Islands. The Fifth Fleet was to begin air strikes and shore bombardment to crush any resistance to the amphibious assault planned for the 15th of June.

We began air operations on the 8th of June, launching our torpedo squadron to attack Japanese ships. As I watched the crews climb into their aircraft, the turret gunner of one of the Avengers shouted, and waved at me.

"Hey, Mr. Hawkins! I told you I'd get on a crew!" he shouted. His name was Turner.

I cupped my hands around my mouth. "Turner, shoot down one for me!" I called back.

Turner gave me a thumbs up as he began strapping in.

Turner was an aircraft armorer, and he was very good at his job. Because I had never had a gun jam anytime he had worked on my plane, I often asked for him.

"Turner," I asked one day, "is it true your name is actually General Turner?"

"Yes, sir," Turner replied as he skillfully laced the ammo belts into the feeding chutes. "General Lee Turner, that's my real name."

I laughed. "You should have gone into the Army. Think what fun you could have by calling someone and telling them you are General Turner."

"Ahh, it would probably just get me in trouble," Turner replied. "Anyway, there'd be some damn Yankee somewhere who wouldn't understand that I was named after General Robert E. Lee. There, that'll take care of you, Mr. Hawkins."

"Thanks," I said.

"You're going to have to find somebody else you trust. I won't be doing this much longer," Turner said.

"Why not?"

"I was checked out as a turret gunner while I was in ordnance school," he said. "I figure to be going on a crew pretty soon."

Shortly after that conversation, we lost some of our pilots and gunners in combat, creating some vacancies, so Turner's application was accepted.

This was his very first mission, and his smile spread from ear to ear as his pilot, Ensign Charley Mantell, was guided into launch position.

Mantell was also a replacement, and though he was carrier qualified, like Turner, this was his first mission.

The launch officer made his little launching dance, winding up in a squatting position with his finger pointed dramatically toward the end of the deck, and Mantell gunned the engine as the catapult thrust it forward.

The Avenger was three thousand pounds heavier than the Hellcat, and because of that, a bit more difficult to launch.

"He doesn't have enough speed!" Stewart said, verbalizing what all of us could tell.

Mantell lifted off, then banked to the right, but he had not attained enough speed and, to compound matters, when he banked, he lost what lift he had. The Avenger sliced into the water on our starboard side and disappeared. I stood on the flight deck hoping to see a survivor, but no one ever surfaced.

It was a sobering moment for us all.

We launched our first fighter sweeps over the islands on the 11th of June. VF 31 launched twelve fighters for a sweep over the bomber base at Ushi Point on the northern tip of Tinian Island. Everyone wanted to go on the mission and we drew straws for it. I was unlucky enough to draw a long straw. The rest of us were kept aboard the *Cabot* in reserve.

As the sweep approached their target, they were jumped by twenty Japanese "Zeros." A dogfight followed that lasted some twenty to thirty minutes, starting at 20,000 feet and going all the way down to 3,000 feet. There were numerous head-on encounters and many of our pilots found themselves in a precarious position with a Zero on their tail. Since the fight brought a large number of aircraft together in a tight airspace, many a friend was able to help his buddy by blasting a Zero off his tail. Smoking and burning aircraft filled the air along with parachutes floating down through the melee.

When the dogfight drew to a close, Fighting 31 had knocked fourteen Zeros out of the air and damaged another twenty planes on the ground with the loss of only one plane. Ensign Whitworth's plane was shot down, but he survived. The destroyer, *USS Caperton*, picked him up after he spent three days floating in his rubber raft. The rescue was not without cost, however. The *Caperton* demanded forty gallons of ice cream from the *Cabot* in return for their pilot, and only half-way joking, we told Whitworth that he could not have any ice-cream until we were re-supplied.

The fighter sweeps and bombing attacks continued for the next four days. Fighting 31 accounted for seven more air-to-air kills, and the cumulative bombing and strafing attacks from Task Force 58 laid waste to the military installations on the islands. The shore bombardment from the battleships, cruisers and destroyers rendered the beach defenses ineffective as D-day arrived.

Angel In The Cockpit

On 15 June 1944 *Operation Forager* began. Two divisions of United States Marines and one division of U.S. Army Infantry stormed ashore on Saipan. With the assault on the Mariannas becoming a reality, the Japanese Navy had to move swiftly and decisively to prop up their crumbling strategic position. It was this maneuver that brought about the largest carrier air battle of all time.

The Japanese Navy was making plans for a decisive action with the Fifth Fleet, but the Mariannas caught them by surprise. They had anticipated an attack on the Carolines or the Palau Islands.

Their plans were quickly altered though, and Operation "A-Go" was launched. On the 13th of June, the Japanese Fleet sailed from their base at Tawi Tawi in the Sulu Archipelago, east of Borneo. They passed through the Philippine Islands via the San Bernardino Strait and joined other fleet elements from the home islands 400 miles east of Samar. The combined fleet set a course for the Mariannas and the U.S. Fifth Fleet.

Our submarines, lurking in the narrow passages through the Philippines, reported the progress of the Japanese fleet after its departure. In addition, our cryptographers had long since broken the Japanese naval code, so that our high level commanders were well aware of the Japanese intentions.

The Japanese plan was to launch their strike aircraft just outside the range of our carrier aircraft. They were able to do this because they had a logistical advantage. They controlled Guam, which meant they did not have to return to their carriers, as we did. Japanese planes could fly in, strike our fleet, and proceed on to Guam. There they could land, refuel, rearm, and strike our fleet again on their return to the carriers.

Additionally, as their carrier strike was coming in from one direction, planes from Guam would strike the American fleet from another quarter, attempting to sow panic and confusion as well as sink ships.

Just before midnight on June 18th, Admiral Raymond Spruance, commander of the Fifth Fleet, received a message from his boss, Admiral Chester Nimitz. The Japanese fleet was 350 miles west-southwest of Saipan. This touched off a hot debate between Spruance and Admiral Marc Mitscher. Mitscher wanted to immediately head Task Force 58.2 toward the Japanese fleet at flank speed. By racing west through the night, we would be in a position to launch a strike at the Japanese by dawn.

It was a bold plan, but Spruance demurred. He did not want to leave the vulnerable troop and supply ships without adequate air protection. His fear was that the Japanese fleet might be able to slip around his flank and attack those unprotected ships.

Finally, upon Mitchner's urging, Spruance relented somewhat. The thin-skinned troop and supply ships were moved a safe distance east of the Mariannas. Then he placed Task Force 58 in a defensive position, west of the Mariannas between the American troops and the oncoming enemy. Task Group 58.7 would form this impromptu battle line, and it was removed from the carrier and posted fifteen miles west of the main fleet. Task Group 58.4, the weakest of the carrier groups, was positioned twelve miles north of the battleships to provide air cover for them. This freed the battleships from the many complicated maneuvers required by the carrier air operations and also gave the battleships the chance to maneuver freely to intercept any Japanese surface ships.

The other three Task Groups, 58.1, 58.2 and 58.3, were formed along a north-south line, some twelve miles apart, aligned with the prevailing winds. All the players were in place and the table was set. With adrenaline running high, we waited for the Japanese attack.

Angel In The Cockpit

While waiting, as much to overcome the nervousness as to pass the time, we had a basketball game in one corner of the hanger deck. I was on the team with Stewart, Hayde, and Galt. The other team consisted of Nooy, Bowie, Anderson, and Loomis. The mechanics had made a hoop for us, and we played half-court. It was a spirited game, all of us had played high school basketball, and I and two others had played some college basketball. We had several people gathered to watch the game, and it is said that quite a bit of money was bet on the outcome.

I was high-point man for our team, with twelve points, but Loomis got eighteen points as his team beat us. There was no way of knowing at the time, of course, but Hayde and Loomis would both be dead within a month.

Just after dawn on June 19, air activity was observed over the island of Guam. Multiple aircraft were detected spreading out in a wide fan. Half an hour later, one of the Japanese planes had located Task Force 58. The pilot radioed in our position, then made a solo attack on one of the destroyers in the screen. That bit of foolhardy bravery cost him his life. It was obvious that this was to be the day of the big battle.

Three four-plane divisions of fighters were launched from the *Cabot* at about 08:00 to join the Combat Air Patrol over Task Group 58.2. When multiple aircraft were detected over Guam, the twelve planes from VF 31, along with other fighters, were sent in that direction to investigate. Eight of our planes failed to make any contacts but one division found more than they bargained for.

Lt. Turner's division found itself all alone when they arrived over Guam. They were suddenly jumped by eight Zeroes. In the furious dogfight that followed all of our planes took damage, but they accounted for six of the Zeroes. Damaged and low on fuel, the four planes headed back toward the *Cabot*.

I stood on the island with several other pilots who were getting ready to launch, and watched the recovery. One of the planes missed the arresting wires. Its right gear collapsed and it came careening across the deck toward the island. I watched as the ground crews scrambled to get out of the way. The plane broke in half, then caught fire, but one of the deck crew fireman climbed onto the wing and pulled the pilot from his cockpit.

The two other divisions were also running low on fuel by this time and they returned as well. After these aircraft were recovered, my division was ordered to join the CAP, or Combat Air Patrol, launching even as the first planes were being refueled. We joined the forty-eight other fighters orbiting over the task groups awaiting the expected attack.

My flight of six aircraft from Fighter Squadron 31 was at 25,000 feet over Task Group 58.2. At about 10:00 AM the battleship *Alabama* reported radar contact with a large flight of enemy aircraft about 130 miles from Task Force 58. The U.S.S. *Cabot* quickly confirmed this contact and forty-two fighters from the Combat Air Patrol, including my flight of six, were vectored toward the enemy.

Almost as soon as the enemy raid had been detected, the entire flight of Japanese planes began a wide 360° turn while the Japanese strike commander gave his pilots instructions. This maneuver gave Task Force 58 time to clear its flight decks and get additional fighter aircraft into the air, and to give the Combat Air Patrol time to intercept the strike much farther away from the carriers. There was also a Japanese interpreter on one of our carriers who was listening to the enemy's aircraft frequency. He was able to hear the briefing being given to the attacking pilots and relay this information to the task force fighter director.

While we were on our way to intercept this raid, the fifteen carriers of Task Force 58 turned into the wind and the fighter scramble began. One-hundred-forty additional fighters were launched in the next fifteen minutes. The dive bombers and torpedo bombers on the decks were launched and told to orbit west of Guam. This was done to keep the decks of the carriers clear, so that the fighter aircraft could land, refuel, rearm and return to the fight during the coming battle. It also removed the danger of armed and fueled aircraft from the flight decks.

After completing their sweeping turn, the enemy flight started to close on Task Force 58. This flight consisted of sixty-four aircraft - a mixture of fighters, dive bombers, and torpedo bombers. At 1035 our Combat Air Patrol flight sighted the enemy force at fifty-five miles from Task Force 58, flying at 18,000 feet. With a 6,000-foot altitude advantage, the first eight of our fighters dove on the enemy formation. They were followed in rapid succession by the remaining aircraft of the flight.

The *Great Mariannas Turkey Shoot* was under way.

My flight rolled into the attack with a seven thousand-foot altitude advantage and joined the dogfight that was in progress. I picked out a lone fighter aircraft that had strayed from his flight. He saw me coming and started a violent turn to engage. He was a little late in starting the turn. With a no-deflection burst from my six .50 caliber machine guns, he broke apart and started down in flames. The excessive speed of my closing dive allowed me to swoop back up to altitude and position myself for another run.

There were many burning airplanes and parachutes in my area of the sky. It was hard selecting another target, especially with so many of our pilots mixing it up in this massive dogfight. The enemy planes had started to lose altitude for some reason and I was able to get another fighter in my gun sights. I followed him through some steep, high "G" turns until he finally leveled out. After a long burst from my guns, he erupted into flames.

I continued into my dive and found myself in a tail chase with another Japanese fighter that was headed for the deck. I closed on him and sent a long burst into the plane from close range. He suddenly cut his power on me and I overran him. I thought I had really gotten myself into deep trouble. But as I pulled up and turned to engage him, I saw that he was already burning and headed for the water. I had shot down three airplanes within a ten-minute time frame.

The enemy formation began to break up under our rapid succession of attacks. I re-entered the dogfight and maneuvered to engage another Zero. As I closed, I was surprised to see tracer fire passing in front of me from my right. I made a violent right turn to engage. When I rolled out of my turn, I found myself head-on with another Hellcat. I didn't know if I had seen friendly tracer fire passing in front of me or that of an enemy Zero. I pulled up and exited.

After only twenty minutes of this fast-moving dogfight, additional aircraft from Task Force 58 started arriving on the scene. The pickings by this time were slim. The surviving enemy aircraft consisted of only a few scattered individual aircraft, still making their way toward their targets.

By this time, I was separated from my flight, getting low on fuel and in need of more ammunition. I checked in with my fighter director and he directed me back to the task force through safe channels. I was ordered to land on the *USS Monterey*, which had a clear deck at the time. After I made my approach and landing, they taxied me forward and placed me on the starboard catapult. I remained in the cockpit as they refueled and rearmed my aircraft.

I sat there strapped into my plane, waiting to be launched back into the battle. Suddenly, I noticed that everyone on the flight deck was taking cover in the catwalks or anywhere they could get under something. I looked up and saw a single enemy aircraft making a dive-bombing run on the *Monterey*. Every ship that could bring their guns to bear was firing at the plane as the bomb was released. I watched the bomb continue its fall – thankfully it hit in the water some distance from the ship. The bomb caused no damage, but fragments from bursting, friendly 5-inch antiaircraft shells started peppering the flight deck like a hailstorm. As those lethal fragments swept the deck, they shot me off the catapult and back into the air to join the ongoing battle.

Some of the enemy aircraft who had escaped being shot down made some uncoordinated single-plane attacks on the battleship task group. One bomb hit near the battleship *South Dakota,* killing twenty-seven men and wounding twenty-three. What was left of the enemy aircraft made their individual ways back to their carriers.

While the first raid was underway, the Japanese launched a second raid. This was a very large raid consisting of a total of eighty torpedo and dive bombers, escorted by forty-eight fighters. The approaching enemy aircraft were detected by radar from the carrier *Lexington* at about 1100, at a range of one-hundred-fifteen miles. As in the first raid, the enemy flight made a large, sweeping turn. Again, this was to allow their Strike Commander to brief them, and again, our forces were monitoring the briefing. As before, the information was furnished to the Force Fighter Director. This, and the time delay, made Task Force 58's interception much easier.

In addition to the planes that had intercepted the first raid, Task Force 58 had one-hundred-twenty-nine more fighters in the air and available to handle this raid. After the radar contact detected enemy planes, thirty-three more fighters were scrambled. The first twelve fighters vectored out to intercept the raid sighted the enemy at about 1139. As in the first raid, our fighters had been given a 5,000-foot altitude advantage. With this advantage, the attack began. In rapid succession additional fighter aircraft joined the rapidly growing dogfight. This fight lasted for about twenty minutes. By then, the surviving enemy aircraft were coming in sight of the battleship task group and were letting down for their attacks.

Not many of the aircraft from this raid survived the initial contact, but a few managed to carry out small attacks against three of the five task groups. Without exception, they were unsuccessful. Our only casualties were from two bombs that made near misses on two of our carriers. The bombs killed three men and wounded eighty-five. Of the one-hundred-twenty-eight aircraft launched by the enemy, only a handful survived.

During that same morning the Japanese launched yet a third raid. This attack force consisted of sixteen fighter aircraft, twenty-six fighter-bomber aircraft and seven torpedo planes. This raid was destined for trouble from its start. The flight was initially directed to a point that was sixty miles to the north of Task Force 58's actual location. While on the way to their targets, a corrected position for Task Force 58 was radioed to the flight. The Japanese fighter aircraft received the message and altered their course to close with Task Force 58, but the torpedo and dive-bombers missed the message and flew on to the original assigned position. They saw no task force and headed back toward their carriers. The sixteen fighter aircraft were detected approaching the task force and a flight of fighters was vectored out to intercept. The enemy was engaged and in a brief dogfight, seven of the enemy planes were shot down without loss to our fighters.

The Japanese launched a fourth raid - their last raid of the day. This raid consisted of thirty fighter aircraft and fifty-two bombers. Like Raid III this raid was destined for trouble. Their strike element was once again given an incorrect position for Task Force 58. After flying to this position and finding no ships, eighteen of the aircraft decided to return to their carrier. The remaining planes decided to split into two flights and land at Guam and Rota. Our forces encountered each of these three flights.

Then, through sheer luck, a three-plane search group from one of our carriers sighted the flight returning to the Japanese carriers. In the encounter that followed, three Japanese planes were shot down. The flight of fifteen dive bombers on their way to land at Rota passed over Task Group 58.2 and delivered an ineffective dive bomb attack. Five of the enemy planes were shot down by antiaircraft fire from the ships.

The remaining flight, totaling forty-nine aircraft, was headed for Guam and Rota. They all arrived over the airfield at Guam and began to circle in preparation for landing. The Japanese planes were greeted by forty-one of our fighter aircraft. Thirty of the forty-nine enemy aircraft were shot down in the traffic pattern, and the remaining nineteen were so damaged by the time they got on the ground that they were no longer air-worthy.

With the shattering of Raid IV, *The Great Mariannas Turkey Shoot* came to a close. The Japanese had thrown 323 of their 430 aircraft against Task Force 58, and 253 of them had been shot out of the air. With the land-based aircraft from the islands shot down, the total air-to-air victories during the *Mariannas Turkey Shoot* climbed to over three hundred. The total cost to Task Force 58 was seven fighter aircraft lost in aerial combat, plus thirty killed and one-hundred-eight wounded in the few attacks that got through to the ships of the task force.

The horrendous loss of planes and pilots was not the only bad news for the Japanese Navy on June 19th. A single torpedo from the American submarine *Albacore* struck the Japanese flagship, the carrier *Taiho*, shortly after she had launched a strike against the US fleet. A fire started near an aviation fuel tank, and aided by inept damage control, spread throughout the ship. The *Taiho* sank before sunset.

Another American submarine, the *Cavalla,* put three torpedoes into the fleet carrier *Shokaku*. The torpedo hits started fires near the bomb magazine. When the conflagration reached the bombs that afternoon, the *Shokaku* blew up and sank.

With these devastating losses of ships, aircraft and pilots, the Japanese Naval Air Arm ceased to be an effective weapon.

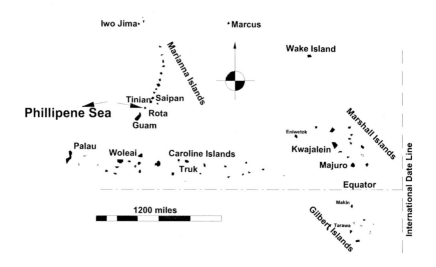

The Great Mariannas Turkey Shoot

Chapter Five

The Battle of the Philippine Sea

The Battle of the Philippine Sea was not a surface battle where you had combat vessels engaging each other with their mounted guns and torpedoes. This battle was one of aircraft against a fleet. The battle came after the successful repulse of the air attacks the Japanese had launched against Task Force 58 during the *Mariannas Turkey Shoot*. Admiral Spruance granted Admiral Mitscher's request to close with the Japanese fleet and launch air strikes against it.

With the last of the Japanese raids, the Turkey Shoot phase of the Battle of the Philippine Sea came to a close at about 1500 on 19 June 1944. Task Force 58 set a course west-southwest to move into range of the Japanese fleet. We steamed through the night of the 19th at flank speed, slowly closing the gap on the enemy.

It was during this nighttime cruise that one on the oddities of the Pacific War happened. The *Cabot* had secured from general quarters and flight quarters. We were planning to settle in for the night while we raced toward the enemy fleet. Our calm was shattered when general quarters sounded, with the call to man all flight quarters stations. Word came over the ship's loud speakers to stand by to land aircraft. A plane had entered the *Cabot's* landing pattern.

Our Landing Signal Officer had sighted the aircraft and begun to give it signals for landing. The pilot in the aircraft responded correctly to all the signals given. But as the plane approached touchdown, you could see the big red ball markings of the Japanese Rising Sun on it wings. The LSO gave a violent wave-off signal, and the plane left the landing pattern and disappeared out to sea. It was tracked by radar for a few miles but at such a low altitude, we soon lost radar contact. We could only surmise that the plane was from one of the Japanese raids of the previous day and had become a straggler. It was obvious that he was lost in the dark and was trying to find his way back to his fleet. In the dark, he had mistaken us for his home carrier. With this excitement over, we did secure to our bunks, while Task Force 58 continued to close on the enemy fleet. We steamed all night and into the following day.

The Japanese fleet took little or no action during this period. They launched no air strikes and neither closed with the American fleet nor ran away from it. The reason for this was their commander. Admiral Ozawa had been forced to transfer to a destroyer when his flagship, the *Taiho*, had been torpedoed the previous day. The destroyer lacked the communications capability necessary to command a modern fleet. It was mid afternoon on the 20th before he transferred to the carrier *Zuikaku* and learned the extent of yesterday's debacle. Still he began to organize another strike in the optimistic belief that there must be hundreds of Japanese combat aircraft still active in the Mariannas.

Around 1540 on the 20th, a contact report came in, indicating that we had closed to within 240 miles of the Japanese fleet. A strike, composed of over 200 aircraft, fighters, dive bombers and torpedo planes, was launched toward the reported location at about 1600. The *Cabot* contributed four TBM torpedo bombers to this raid.

> The **TBM** was the newest American torpedo bomber. It had originally been the **TBF** and built by Grumman, but the needs of wartime production caused many to be built by General Motors and designated TBM. The aircraft had decent armament and speed, good bomb capacity and excellent range. The only drawback to it was defective torpedoes that plagued it until late 1944.

Our fighters were held back to guard the task force. After the flight was already on its way, a revised radar plot ascertained that the enemy fleet was sixty miles farther out than the first estimated position. With this information, Admiral Mitscher knew that our aircraft would be returning in the dark and low on fuel. A second planned strike against the enemy fleet was canceled and preparations were made to recover our returning strike aircraft in the dark.

My four-plane division was launched at the same time as the strike. We were assigned to high altitude Combat Air Patrol, 25,000 feet over Task Group 58.2. We were also to act as radio relay between the strike aircraft and the command ships. At our altitude we could keep radio contact with the strike aircraft almost all the way to the target.

We listened as the pilots received word that the flight had been extended by sixty miles. There was much discussion on methods of fuel conservation to allow them to make their attack and return to their carriers. It was mutually decided that there would be no time to loiter over target for damage assessment or repeated attacks. There was also much chatter between pilots along the lines of, "Who was the dumb so-and-so who made the first estimate of the enemy's position?" or words to that effect.

The strike passed out of radio range and we gradually lost contact. We flew in tense silence while our friends approached the target and made their attack on the enemy fleet. We were in the dark, with no real idea about what was going on. We could only wait until our aircraft turned for home and came back into radio range. Then we would learn the results of the attack and how much fuel they had left.

Around 1930 we began to hear radio chatter from the returning aircraft. We heard one pilot say, "Man, did you see that antiaircraft fire. It was all colors - red, white, yellow and green. They must have been trying to shoot us down with a rainbow."

Another pilot exclaimed, "Did you see that carrier burning? I saw at least five hits on its deck. It can't last more that twenty minutes!"

There was chatter from the fighter pilots about mixing it up with the Japanese Zeros and chatter from the dive bomber pilots talking of attacks on the enemy battleships and carriers. One pilot piped up with, "That antiaircraft fire was so thick you could walk on it."

Based on all this radio chatter, the attack appeared to be a smashing success and we reported this to the carriers. Final analysis and evaluation could only come after the recovery of the planes and the debriefing of the flight crews. Along with the talk of a successful attack came chatter about the critical fuel situation aboard most of the aircraft.

We heard the chatter from one particular flight of six dive-bombers. The flight leader discussed their fuel state with the other pilots of the flight. They determined that they did not have enough fuel to reach their home carrier. The flight leader ordered all six planes to land in the water, in close proximity to each other. Each crew would abandon their aircraft and inflate their rubber rafts. Then they would rendezvous, tie the rafts together and await rescue. We listened as the flight leader said, "One hundred feet to touch down, keep it smooth and good luck." Then there was silence.

We heard many other radio reports from the pilots, such as, "She's starting to sputter; I'm taking her in," and one transmission that simply said, "Dave, if I don't make it back, tell Mae I love her."

Other radio messages reported that the pilots were having difficulty receiving the homing signals from the fleet. We reported this to the flagship. It was then that Admiral Mitscher earned a place in the hearts of carrier pilots for all time.

As the evening twilight deepened into night, Admiral Mitscher ordered the carriers to turn on their running lights. He also directed a number of ships to turn on their searchlights and point them up to the skies or to fire star shells to illuminate the area. This gave the returning pilots a position of the fleet and allowed them to locate their home carriers for landing.

This decision was a courageous one, made during a battle in time of war. These lights not only gave our position to the pilots - they also gave it to any enemy submarines that might be in the area. This was a bold decision on the Admiral Mitscher's part and I will tell you one thing, it certainly endeared him to the pilots who were alone in the dark, low on fuel and frantically searching for their home carrier.

We could tell from the radio chatter that the returning pilots could not only pick up the searchlights, but could also see the star shells being fired from the fleet. This brought about jubilant comments such as, "Hooray! There she is - home base! We're on our way!"

We learned later that Admiral Mitscher had made the decision to turn on the lights earlier in the day. It was not something he had decided at that last minute. He had also ordered all carriers of Task Force 58 to take aboard any airplane from the strike that entered their landing pattern.

Those of us in the Combat Air Patrol and Radio Relay were ordered to land when the planes of the strike reentered direct radio range. We set down quickly and our aircraft were immediately taken below to the hangar deck. All flight decks in the task force were cleared and readied to receive the returning aircraft.

As planes started arriving in the dark with drying fuel tanks the situation edged toward mass confusion. It was not uncommon to have two to three planes coming up the grove for landing at the same time. The abundance of lights was confusing to some of the pilots - it was hard to pick out the carriers. It was not unusual to see a plane making an aborted approach on one of the destroyers.

There were some cases of a plane being safely on deck, waiting to clear the arresting gear. A plane in the grove behind them would receive a wave-off and not have enough fuel to go around. The dying engine would cause the plane to crash right on top of the plane on the deck. There were many cases of planes in the landing pattern running out of fuel and ditching in the water alongside one of the screening destroyers. It was a hectic half-hour until the last plane was aboard or accounted for. The lights were turned off at about 2250.

As ordered, pilots landed on any carrier they could find. The *Cabot* took aboard seven aircraft from other air groups. This filled our decks to capacity. After that we would extract the pilot and crew from any other planes that landed and push the aircraft over the stern to clear the deck for the next landing.

We had one comic moment. As one plane was being pushed over the stern to clear the deck, a sailor was seen in the cockpit. He was working frantically to remove the aviation clock from the instrument panel for a souvenir. We lucked out and removed *him* before the plane got the deep six. I never did find out if he got the clock.

When the last aircraft was aboard, all effort turned to rescue. Screening destroyers picked up the pilots and crews that had ditched in the water around the force. Then Admiral Mitscher further endeared himself to the flyers by putting the four task groups of Task Force 58 in a line-abreast formation that covered some twenty miles and ordering a course back along the route the strike aircraft had flown on their return. We steamed on this course all night picking up pilots and crews.

At first light we launched search aircraft to cover the entire area. We were not only looking for the Japanese, but we were also looking for any pilots and crews that were missed in the night. Thanks to this massive fleet rescue mission, our losses for this phase of the Battle of the Philippine Sea were kept to sixteen pilots and thirty-three crewmen.

We eventually got all four of our TBM air crews back. Two of the planes had attacked the carrier *Chiyoda*. They both managed to return to the *Cabot* with less than five gallons of fuel remaining. The other two struck a *Kongo* class battleship. One of these planes landed on *the USS Bunker Hill* but the plane was wrecked in the landing. The other crew was forced to ditch, but they were rescued by the destroyer *Hunt* and returned on the 22nd.

Along with the search planes we had a strike ready to launch on the 21st. Even some of our fighters were going to be used to deliver 500-pound bombs. When we found the Japanese fleet, it was a disappointment. They were at least one hundred miles out of range. Admiral Ozawa had been ordered to withdraw and he was running hard. We would get no chance to finish off the Japanese that day.

Debriefing the strike pilots showed that one large carrier had surely been sunk. Two light carriers had received bomb hits and were left burning. Two battleships were damaged and left on fire. One fleet oiler had definitely been sunk and one had been left burning.

Some of our pilots were frustrated and disappointed with these results since we did not deliver a crushing blow to the enemy carriers. Six of the Japanese flat tops were still afloat and might return to battle once again. This disappointment was somewhat relieved when we learned that our submarines had accounted for two Japanese carriers. We also knew that the Japanese would not have enough qualified pilots to man the remaining flight decks since some 300 pilots had been lost in the Mariannas.

After the battle, it took time to get airplanes and pilots back to their home carriers. Replacement aircraft were flown in from "Jeep Carriers" that were in the area with spare aircraft aboard. We left the Saipan area on June 23rd, heading back to out new fleet anchorage in the Kwajalein Atoll. On the way, we passed close to Pagan Island, farther north in the Mariannas. We pounded the Japanese installations there with guns and bombs, leaving them a wreck. We reached Kwajalein on June 27th.

Between June 1st and June 23rd, VF 31 had shot down 45 Japanese aircraft without the loss of a single pilot – quite a good tally.

We had been living a charmed life. In our first six months of combat Fighting 31 had shot down sixty-four Japanese planes without the loss of a single pilot. On June 29th we sustained our first casualty, and you could say it was from friendly fire.

Lieutenant Commander Robert A. Winston had been our squadron commander ever since the early days back in New Jersey. Now, suddenly, he was gone. When we arrived

Angel In The Cockpit

at the anchorage, orders came through promoting him to full commander and transferring him back to the Navy Department in Washington DC. It was a blow to lose someone who had shared lives with us for more than a year but we said our goodbyes and moved on.

Our new commander was Lieutenant Commander Daniel J. Wallace, Jr. He certainly had the credentials for a naval aviator. An Annapolis graduate, he had served with VF-10 aboard the *Enterprise* and been executive officer of VF-14 aboard the *Wasp*. He had very little time to settle in because Task Force 58 was shortly at sea once more and headed for the enemy.

On our way back to the Mariannas to support the landings on Guam, we struck Iwo Jima a crushing blow. Iwo Jima was one of a long string of rough volcanic islands called the Bonin's, lying between the Mariannas and Japan. We hit Iwo Jima and Chichi Jima with all our air power and the surface ships of Task Group 58.7 shelled the islands heavily. These strikes on Iwo Jima served a twofold purpose. The first was to ensure that no raids were flown out of Iwo Jima against our operations in the Mariannas. The second could be classified as initial strikes to soften up Iwo Jima for the planned occupation of the island at a later date. Appropriately enough, the fireworks began on July 4th.

The fighters of VF-31 were scheduled for Combat Air Patrol over the islands. Half took off at dawn to go in with the first strikes while the rest of us would join the fight in mid-morning. The three fighter divisions from the *Cabot* were assigned to fly "top cover" at 15,000 feet. They maintained their assigned position and watched the action unfolding below them. Bombers from the Task Force were pounding the airfields on Iwo Jima. They could also see some of their comrades tangling with Japanese fighters at a lower altitude. A portion of the Combat Air Patrol was sent into that fight but the VF-31 planes remained as high cover.

They also noticed a flight of perhaps thirty Japanese fighters moving off to the north as if they were fleeing the battle. Our pilots looked longingly at the fleeing targets as they drew out of sight. Once safely out of sight, these planes climbed to 20,000 feet and turned back south. Minutes later, they dove out of the sun right into the midst of the VF-31 flight.

Our fighters ran into a hornet's nest. The Japanese pilots were from a top line unit of the Japanese Army and they flew the fast, deadly Army fighter labeled the Tojo.

In the chaotic, swirling dogfight that followed, our pilots shot down fifteen aircraft, had two probables and damaged four others. Every one of our planes sustained damage. Several of the nine that returned to the *Cabot* were no longer airworthy. Three planes, and their pilots: Malcom Loomis, Haig Elezian, and Frank Hancock did not return. We had suffered our first air-to-air casualties. Later, when we found out who we had lost, I couldn't help but think about Loomis and the basketball game we had played on the hangar deck.

My division took off about 1000 in the first of three combat flights over the islands. We were in support of, and air cover for, the shore bombardment, and the bombing and strafing of military installations in the area. To our disappointment, no more Japanese aircraft came up to oppose us. We also looked for any sign of our lost pilots, hoping to see a bright yellow raft floating in the ocean, awaiting rescue. Our search was fruitless.

With sadness in our hearts, we retired from the Bonin Islands with the conviction that we would return one day. Task Force 58 sailed south toward Guam to support the landings there.

We hit the Japanese airfields on Rota hard on July 7th, bombing and strafing the fields and hangars. The following day,

Angel In The Cockpit

VF-31 was split into thirds to provide Combat Air Patrol over the other missions. Our first eight planes took off at dawn but saw no enemy aircraft in the sky. Our second flight intercepted a flight of six Japanese planes from Guam and shot them all down. My turn came in the afternoon.

We were on a Combat Air Patrol mission, orbiting high above the action below when we spotted a flight of three Zeros trying to escape the destruction going on at Guam. We dove on them, and I downed one Zero in a one-on-one dogfight. My flight accounted for the other two. That was my fifth air-to-air kill. I was barely twenty-one and now I was an ace.

There was no time to rest on my laurels though, as we continued our bombing and strafing Guam, Rota and Tinian for the next two weeks. We had to soften them up for the planned amphibious landings.

Our division was scheduled to fly early morning Combat Air Patrol on the 15th of July but the weather was so bad that our launch was delayed. We were in the middle of a fierce thunderstorm with driving rain, a violently pitching deck and almost no visibility. At about 0600 the radar spotted a bogey headed toward the task group and we launched, weather or not.

Our flight joined up and started a climb through the storm. The flight leader, Lieutenant Stewart, had some instrument problems and turned over the lead to my friend and roommate, Lieutenant (jg) Frank Hayde. We climbed through the howling darkness and finally broke clear of the storm at 20,000 feet. But Frank never made it through. We looked around and called on the radio but there was no sign of him. Ships and planes of the task group searched, but no wreckage was ever found. The final verdict was that Frank had become disoriented in the gloom of the storm and flown his plane into the ocean. I mourned for Frank, as I had mourned for my own brother.

Two days later we lost one of our replacement pilots in the same way, a young ensign who had only been with the squadron for ten days. It was hard on all of us, but there were other missions that had to be accomplished. There were islands to be bombed and invaded before we would reach the Japanese homeland. So, with our resolve strengthened by the memory of our fallen friends, we carried on.

Eight months of island hopping had brought us two thousand miles across the Central Pacific, from the Marshalls to the Mariannas. Advances in New Guinea and the occupation of Hollandia had paved the way. We were almost ready for the long-awaited assault on the Philippines.

The initial part of the plan was to mount an invasion of the island of Peleliu in the Palau Island chain. This would give us a base of operation almost at the front door of the Philippines. In addition, the Navy would seize Ulithi Atoll to provide a convenient and secure fleet anchorage.

On the 28th of July, we struck the island of Yap, located between the Mariannas and the Palau chain. Our planes did not encounter serious opposition in the air but the ground fire was intense. We had a scare when two of our pilots didn't make it back to the *Cabot,* but both were picked up by destroyers and thankfully returned to us.

On the first of August we anchored off Saipan to rearm and refit. We did not stay there very long. A reconnaissance plane spotted a Japanese convoy near Chichi Jima with supplies and reinforcements for the Mariannas and we headed north to stop them.

We moved in for a return engagement in the Bonin Island chain with due caution. On one flight my division of four aircraft caught a light cruiser trying to hide in a steep, narrow inlet. The weather and the cliffs bordering this fjord made the attack on the

Angel In The Cockpit

cruiser very dangerous but we carried through, even under those adverse conditions.

We had been taught the art of skip bombing back in training. This type of attack calls the attacking plane to fly in toward the target low on the water. When you arrive at the proper distance from the target, the bomb is released. With its forward speed, the bomb will skip off the water and bury itself into the side of the target ship.

As we skip bombed the enemy light cruiser the antiaircraft fire was very intense. We were able to minimize the effect of this fire by popping out of the low cloud ceiling, making our run in, releasing our bombs and popping back into the cloud cover as we made our escape. Later in the day a photo flight reported the cruiser smoking badly and down by the stern.

Aircraft releases bomb and evades.

Skip Bombing

Bomb skips off water & into target.

On our mission the second day, we spotted three large landing craft manned and underway. Our attack left them all burning and dead in the water. We called in gunfire from one of our destroyers to finish them off. With these two days of strikes, our bombing squadron had sunk a 3,000-ton supply ship and a Japanese Fubuki-class destroyer, while severely damaging another large supply ship. All told, Task Force 58 bagged four large cargo ships, the light cruiser, three destroyers and a large number of barges and smaller craft.

While we were in the neighborhood, we plastered Chichi Jima and Iwo Jima once again. After our furious greeting last time, the opposition was disappointing. The planes of VF-31 did not see any enemy planes in the air during our missions, but the ground fire was heavy and the weather was lousy requiring us to attack under a low overcast.

After the strikes on Iwo Jima and Chichi Jima, Task Force 58 made its way back south to complete the loading of supplies and rearming. We were scheduled to cover the landings on Peleliu in early September. First though, we had another matter to complete.

The commander of the South Pacific's Third Fleet, Admiral William F. "Bull" Halsey drew up the operational plans for the assault on the Philippines. To implement these plans, command of our fleet was transferred from Admiral Spruance to Admiral Halsey. At this point, the Fifth Fleet became the Third Fleet and our carrier, the Cabot, was now in Task Group 38.2. Scuttlebutt had it that this change of fleet numbers was done to confuse the Japanese - making them think we had two large fleets. This was not the case though, as there were only two fleet staffs. One staff was conducting the present operation. "The drivers change, but the horses remain the same. Landings on Peleliu began on 6 September 1944, and lasted for two days. My division flew two combat missions. We strafed and bombed the troops and gun positions on the island. The amphibious operations went smoothly with a minimum of opposition. The atoll of Ulithi had been seized and was being readied as a fleet anchorage. The operation was proceeding as planned when we broke off our attacks on the Palau Islands and turned toward Mindanao.

We were ordered to mount three or four days of strikes against the bases and airfields on the large southernmost Philippine island of Mindanao. We would then pull back, replenish, refuel, rearm and move up to the central Philippine islands: Samar, Leyte and Negros. We would launch strikes against them for three or four days. This type of operation would be continued all the way through the northern island of Luzon. Task Force 38's mission was to support the landings on Peleliu by neutralizing all the enemy installations in this area that could interfere. What we did not know, at the time, was that these strikes were also the beginning of a softening up operation that would lead to the assault of MacArthur's forces on the beaches of Leyte.

We began the attacks on Mindanao with little or no air opposition. The Cabot launched mixed flights of fighters and bombers all day. We pounded the airfields first; then we began to look for other targets.

On one flight during these strikes, my division attacked a group of ships that were underway. As we dove through heavy antiaircraft fire, I picked out a 500 ton freighter as my target. Even though the only ordnance I had were my six .50 caliber guns, I sprayed the ship from stem to stern. I was certainly surprised when the entire ship exploded into one large mushroom cloud and sank. The ship was obviously loaded with ammunition, and one of my incendiary bullets must have set it off.

On another flight during these strikes on Mindanao, I caught a patrol boat underway. I was able to stop him dead in the water and leave him in flames. We accomplished our mission of neutralizing any military bases on Mindanao. After a pullback and replenishment, we turned our attention to the central islands of the Philippines, namely Leyte, Cebu, Bohol and Negros, all had major military installations and airfields.

On one strike, my division was assigned to fly protection for a flight of bombers that were to hit the airfields on Negros Island. The flight consisted of thirty-six bombers and twelve fighters. The nine divisions of four bombers each would fly in close formation, which gave their rear-seat gunners proper coverage to repel an air attack on the formation. The three divisions, of four fighters each, would fly high, medium and low cover over the bomber formation. One division would fly a weaving pattern at 5,000 feet above the formation. Another division would fly the same type pattern at 2,000 feet above the formation. The third division would split up and form a box around the bombers at the same altitude. My division was assigned to this "low cover" position.

As the strike approached the target, two fighter planes, Japanese Oscars, attacked us. They came from above in almost a vertical dive. They passed through the formation firing, but caused no damage. The commander for our flight came on the radio and released my section from low cover and said, "Go get 'em, Stew."

Lieutenant James Stewart, "Stew", was my section leader and we immediately flipped into a split "S" and pulled onto the tail of the two Oscars.

We followed them down to the deck. At our tremendous speed, Stew over ran the first Oscar and had to pull up and reposition himself. I had slowed my speed and was in perfect position for a burst from my six .50 caliber guns. We were so low that when the bullets from my guns hit, it forced the "Oscar" into the ground. The plane bounced back into the air and exploded into flames.

I had lost contact with Stew at some point during the fight. Now, I broke left and gained altitude to find myself alone, directly over an airfield. There were aircraft taking off below me to join their comrades already in the air. At about 2,000 feet over the field, I settled on the tail of an Oscar and with a quick burst from my guns, sent him spinning into the ground in flames.

I did a pull up into a high wing-over maneuver and headed back toward the airfield. I met another Oscar head-on, coming at me with his guns blazing. As we played "chicken," the fire from my six .50 caliber guns literally tore the engine right off his aircraft. I made a violent right turn to avoid a head-on collision. As I completed my turn to continue engagement, I saw the Oscar strike the ground, billowing black smoke.

I received a radio call from Stew telling me to get over to the second airfield where planes were taking off. I wasn't sure which field I was over at the time, so I headed west knowing the airfields were more or less on that line.

On my way to join up with Stew, a two-plane section of Oscars made a pass at me. I saw them coming and pulled hard into them. I do not know why they were not firing at me, even though they were approaching a good firing position. I held down my trigger and they flew directly through my line of fire. I could see hits on both of the planes but I was unable to see if either flamed or crashed into the ground. I was so busy trying to get joined up with Stew that I couldn't take time to confirm the outcome.

Things picked up immediately, anyway. I saw tracers crossing in front of me as an Oscar took a ninety-degree deflection shot at me. His speed was such that he over-ran me and he made a violent turn to come back at me. This put him in a terrible position, as he sat right in my gun sight. A short burst from my guns, and he burst into flames and spun toward the ground.

I continued over the field at low altitude, when explosions started going off everywhere around me. It didn't take long to figure out that the bombers we had been escorting for the strike had arrived and were blowing the hell out of the airfields. I climbed for altitude, settled at about 2,500 feet and started watching the bombing results on the airfield.

While my attention was focused on the action below, I committed the cardinal sin of a fighter pilot - I forgot to always keep my "six-o'clock" covered and my head on a swivel. As I sat there enjoying the show and waiting for someone to get brave enough to take off, someone tapped me on the shoulder and said, "You better look over to your right."

Obviously, since the Hellcat is a single-seat airplane, there was nobody in the cockpit to tap me on the shoulder, but I felt the tap, and heard the words as surely as if I were sitting in the ready room and someone had come up behind me.

It was Guy.

I turned, as Guy had directed, and there was the most beautiful airplane I had ever seen.

It was an Oscar, painted in the markings of one of the famous Japanese Marine Fighter Squadrons. It was green with the red ball of the Rising Sun on the side with pendants of red running from each side of the sun, fore and aft. The plane was waxed and polished until it glistened in the bright sunlight. Obviously the pilot and crew chief of that plane took great pride in it.

The Oscar sat ahead and to the right of me, with an altitude advantage of about 1,500 feet. This was what a fighter pilot calls a perfect position for a high side run on an enemy.

Why he had not made his pass and ended up on my tail is a mystery. It could have been that he was admiring the brand new shiny black F6F-5 Hellcat that I was flying, in just the same manner I was admiring his Oscar. I knew he could out turn me if I challenged him, and I knew I was too low to try and dive away from him. So taking my only out, I turned violently toward him.

He was late in answering my turn, so I got the jump on him. As we met in the middle of the turn I was passing under the belly of his airplane. I had pressed and was holding my trigger down

Angel In The Cockpit

as he flew right through my line of fire, with the bullets ripping his underside. We came out in a violent turn back into each other. His cockpit burst into flames and the plane fell off into a steep dive, headed straight into the ground. Knowing the turning radius of both aircraft, he would have been able to finish me off in less that two or three turns, so I was lucky to have gotten the jump on him and riddled his underside on our first pass.

That was my fifth kill in a single day, and there might have been two more, though I was unable to confirm them.

Through radio contact, my section leader, Stew, and I were able to get back together and head back for the Cabot. Stew had managed to shoot down four Oscars during the melee, even though he had received some damage from the concussion of one of the bombs being dropped on the field. He, too, was low over the field when the bombs started exploding. The total air-to-air victories for our four-plane division on this strike grew to twelve. Our second section had remained to furnish low cover for the bombers, and they shot down three.

Task Force 38 continued strikes on the central islands of the Philippines and gave support, as needed, to the Peleliu occupation. The next phase of the operation called for our emphasis to shift north to military targets on the island of Luzon.

As the attacks got underway, my division was assigned the first strike into Luzon - a predawn fighter sweep against a major airfield, once known as Clark Field. A fighter sweep is designed to launch a flight of fighter aircraft early enough in the morning hours to arrive over the target airfield before sunup. Each fighter is loaded with a 500-pound bomb. They are to sweep in low over the enemy airfield and release their bombs on the runways. The bomb damage is to prevent any enemy aircraft from taking off during the strike. The fighters then gain altitude over the airfield and attack any enemy aircraft that may have gotten into the air.

As advertised, our fighter sweep took off in the pre-dawn darkness and proceeded to Clark Field. We arrived at a little before sunrise and came in low to drop our bombs on the runways. As we were pulling up for altitude, I spotted a Japanese Val dive-bomber trying to make a getaway from the action. I banked left, fell in behind the Val and gave a short burst from my guns. The bullets tore into the left wing and the pilot climbed out on the right wing to bail out. Staying behind, I watched him jump. I then gave the Val another burst from my guns and it exploded and tore apart, requiring a violent maneuver to miss the flying debris. This brought my total to eleven.

> The Val, or Aichi D3A1, was the mainstay of the Japanese carriers in the early part of the war. This dive-bomber is credited with sinking more allied ships than any other Japanese plane. By 1942 it was showing its age and was replaced by the newer and faster Asahi D4Y1, Judy. By 1944 it had been relegated to second line units and land based assignments. Although old and slow, Vals turned out in great numbers to defend the Philippines.

I climbed for altitude and joined my flight. As we were orbiting over the field, waiting for something to happen, a big, four-engine flying boat, an Emily, was observed coming straight into Clark Field from the direction of the sea.

Needless to say, in about two minutes there were Hellcats all over him and he was history. As this bit of combat was going on, we were jumped by a flight of Japanese Zeros who had evidently launched from another field and come to defend against our attack. A whirling dogfight began over Clark Field. Planes were going in all directions and trails of light from tracer bullets were filling the air.

Angel In The Cockpit

I got a snap burst from my guns, into one of the Zeros as we met head on. I pulled up into a tight climbing turn, but could not spot the Zero, nor could I tell what happened to him. In looking for another Zero to tangle with, I spotted a formation of twelve transport aircraft, codenamed Topsys, flying directly below me. I left the dogfight and settled in behind the Topsys. I flamed one and he left the formation in a dive toward the ground. I moved over to the next Topsy and with a short burst, tore a wing off. He spun out of the formation, burning.

> The Topsy, or Mitsubishi Ki-57, was a twin-engine transport plane carrying a crew of four and up to eleven passengers.

About then, I caught sight of a fighter, a Tony, making a 90-degree deflection pass on me. I did a sharp turn into him just before he started firing and got off a short burst as we passed each other. His tracer bullets fell behind me and as I turned back, I saw him disappear into a cloud, trailing smoke.

> The Tony, or Kawasaki Kl 43 Hein (Swallow), was a fast, maneuverable fighter that entered service with the Japanese Army during the war. It was the first Japanese fighter designed with self-sealing fuel tanks and pilot armor – incorporating the lessons learned from the tough, survivable, allied planes it opposed. This nimble fighter could be a deadly opponent in the hands of a trained pilot.

I returned to the Topsy flight and there were friendly fighters just torching them off, one-by-one. I spotted a straggler that had wandered away from the flight as if trying to make his escape. I pulled in behind and blew him out of the sky. He was number fourteen.

Again an enemy fighter, this time a Zero, made an almost vertical firing run on me, but his shots went way out in front of me. I think he thought that I was going much faster than I was. Having been holding position behind the Topsys, I was at a fairly slow speed. The Zero had to pull out quickly from his vertical dive, as we were very close to the ground working on the Topsys. As he pulled up, I followed him and got off one short burst. But with the tremendous speed built up from his dive, I could not catch him. I could not tell if I had done any damage, so I decided I had better get out of there and head for my home base. I was getting low on fuel, and I was sure my ammunition was about depleted. I joined with another member of my flight, and we returned to the Cabot.

Our strikes continued on targets in the Philippines, and the occupation of Peleliu was successfully completed. The new fleet anchorage was established in Ulithi atoll, and it was there that the Cabot anchored on 4 October 1944. After nine months of combat, air group 31 was to be relieved by Air Group 29. Our air group would leave the Cabot and go aboard the USS Barnes. Then we would return to the states for leave and reassignment. We were certainly elated to be returning home for some leave with our families, but there was also sadness in leaving all our comrades on the Cabot and knowing we were going to miss the final assault and occupation of the Philippines. However, we were leaving with a feeling of accomplishment. In our nine months of combat we had amassed a record that we all could be proud of.

Little did we know that no other air group would exceed that record during the entire war. Neither did we know that some of us would train and reform the air group and be aboard the carrier, USS Monterey, on our way back to the combat zone only five months later. We said our good-byes, and the song went up, "San Francisco here we come right back where we started from."

Angel In The Cockpit

As air group 31 was preparing for our return to the States, the Cabot issued the following news release for our hometown newspapers:

A flying Meataxe was selected as the VF-31 insignia, with the motto, "Cut 'em Down!"

The "Meat Ax Squadron"

More than 10 Japanese planes per man – that's the destruction record in aerial combat for the Hellcat pilots of the U.S. Navy's "Meat Ax Squadron," Fighting 31.

LT. James S. STEWART of Beverly Hills, California has nine planes to his credit and led a four-plane unit during nine months of Pacific operations. LT. John L. WIRTH, Gary, Indiana, and LT(jg) Arthur R. HAWKINS, Lufkin, Texas, have downed 14 enemy planes each.

LT. STEWART'S division, the SIXTH, has suffered one loss, LT(jg) Frank R, HAYDE, of Kansas City, Missouri. HAYDE shot down six enemy planes, one of the top squadron scores at the time. Ensign Jerome L. WOLF, Sedalia, Missouri, who was with the division in its last action, shot down one enemy aircraft.

The fighter pilot division amassed the bulk of their score in the first carrier attacks on the Philippines. In a single fight on 13 September, the division destroyed 12 Japanese fighters in the air, damaged several others and burned a twin-engine bomber on the ground. On a bombing mission several days later, the men managed to knock 10 Japanese aircraft down, including four twin-engine planes, while bombing and strafing targets.

LT. CMDR D. J. WALLACE, Jr. of Hoboken, New Jersey, the second Commanding Officer of air group 31, said, "When Japs are in the air, STEWART's men are always the first to jump them. It's uncanny, they often have every enemy Jap in the air burning before other fighters reach the action."

"On one attack, STEWART and HAWKINS ran into a flight of Jap fighters taking off to intercept our bombers." WALLACE continued, "HAWKINS shot down five and damaged three, and STEWART destroyed four in the air."

"They met the Japs under any condition, down low where the highly maneuverable Zero had the advantage, or they followed through on head-on runs until they could literally see the whites in the Jap pilots' eyes. Once, STEWART engaged and destroyed an enemy fighter after his engine had been damaged by a bomb blast", WALLACE said.

The Battle of the Eastern Philippines gave the "SIXTH" its first opportunity to meet the highly touted Japanese carrier pilots. Intercepting the huge attacking force, the four Hellcats brought down 13 Jap planes, with WIRTH alone bagging four.

"Their total score looks pretty impressive, but there's more to it than the number of planes shot down," continued WALLACE. "For instance, while we were under attack off Truk, HAWKINS deliberately flew through all the ack-ack our Task Force could throw up, to bring down a Jap torpedo bomber that was attacking the Force."

Ensign WOLF, the new division member, had shot down two planes before joining 31. The 43 planes shot down by the four members of STEWART'S division help make up the 147 total destroyed in the air by the "Meat Ax Squadron," and that's a top record for any carrier unit its size. WALLACE and WINSTON's air group 31 also accounted for 26 ships sunk and 22 damaged or probably sunk during the nine months of combat duty.

For the moment, my "time travel" was over, and I found myself back in the present at the Naval Air Museum in Pensacola,

Angel In The Cockpit

Florida. Sometimes, you can start thinking about a song and it begins running in a loop so that you can't get it out of your head. As I sat there in the now ancient Hellcat on the floor of the Naval Air Museum, the tune and refrain of "San Francisco" played over and over in my mind.

I sighed, slid the canopy open, then climbed down from the plane. The ghosts of the place were never more alive than they were at that moment.

Chapter Six

I Have Returned

When I got home that night, I told my wife about my little "time travel" episode, while sitting in the cockpit of the Naval Air Museum's Hellcat.

"It's hard to explain, Louise," I said. "But, while I was sitting in that cockpit, it was as if I were actually reliving the war. I could see it, hear it, smell it, feel it, and taste it. When I climbed down, it was almost as if I were about to go to the pilots' ready room."

"You should write about it," Louise suggested.

I laughed.

"Why are you laughing? I'm serious."

"Come on, Louise, what could I say, that hasn't already been said? There has been so much written about the war. What could I possibly write that is new?"

"It doesn't have to be new; it just has to be personal," Louise said.

"What do you mean?"

"Hawk, there has been a lot written about the Civil War too. But don't you wish you had an account, in his own hand, of your great grandfather's experiences during that time?" Louise asked.

"Yes," I agreed.

"Then, think what a treat your personal experiences will be for your grandchildren and great-grandchildren. Yes, they will know about World War II, no doubt they will study it in history classes, but to them, it will be as remote as the Civil War is to you. But, if they have a personal account from someone who sent through it, and not just someone, but their own flesh and blood relative, then it will come alive for them."

"I don't know," I said. "I'll need to think about it."

"While you are thinking about it, think about some of the specific incidents."

"That was sixty years ago. How am I going to recall specific incidents from sixty years ago?"

"Didn't you say that while you were in the cockpit of the Hellcat, it was all real to you?"

"I did say that. But I can't be climbing into the cockpit all the time. People will think I've gone nuts," I said with a little laugh.

"Hawk, you spend your days in the most complete Naval Aviation Museum in the world. You are surrounded by artifacts from that era."

I thought about what she said and realized that it was true. I didn't have to climb back into the Hellcat to relive that part of my life. I could find a "time portal" almost anywhere in the museum. I slipped, very easily, back to that point in time where my memories had left off the day before.

None of us knew just what the air group's orders to return to the States meant to us individually. We knew that each of us would receive further orders, but to go where, or do what, we did not know. At this point it did not matter much anyway. There was one thing we knew for sure. We were going home for some needed rest and relaxation.

Angel In The Cockpit

The *Cabot* anchored in the Ulithi Atoll in the first week of October 1944. Our air group was scheduled to begin disembarkation from the *Cabot* right away but a typhoon was forming in the area. The normally calm Ulithi anchorage was filled with rough wind and heavy seas.

The effects of this storm made it almost impossible for the air group to transfer into the large boat that had come alongside to ferry us over to our ride home. After many hours fighting the great waves, the heavy gear was loaded into the boat. Every man of the air group had to crawl over the side of the *Cabot* and down heavy cargo netting, just like the infantry we had seen climbing into landing craft for so many island invasions. The crew helped us make the perilous leap into the pitching boat below. I am happy to report that all this was accomplished without the loss of anyone, and we gained a new respect for the men who did this on a regular basis.

The boat took us across choppy waters to the USS *Barnes*, which was anchored in the harbor some distance away. We had to reverse the procedure and load all our equipment and personnel onto the *Barnes*. The choppy waters continued to make the process nearly impossible.

We found out later that this heavy weather was but a prelude to the violent storm that would engulf the Third Fleet later in the month. The typhoon severely damaged the forward decks of several aircraft carriers and resulted in many aircraft lost or damaged. This fierce storm caused many deaths in the Third Fleet when three destroyers were lost. They rolled over and capsized taking their crews down with them. We did not learn of these tragedies until our return to the States.

All hands aboard were elated to be going home, but the journey was not a "bed of roses". The *Barnes* was a small "Jeep" carrier that would normally run with a wartime crew of around

1,200 men. Jeep carriers were not very large to begin with. This one was only about half the size of the *Cabot*. The Jeep or Escort carriers were intended to transport aircraft from port to port, provide minimal air cover for merchant convoys, and support the combat fleet with spare planes. They did this job admirably, but they were small and slow compared to the fleet carriers.

In addition to our air group there were a number of combat weary Marines on their way home, and many fleet personnel being rotated back to the States for emergency leave or reassignment. All told, we added about 1,000 extra bodies to the complement of the ship. All the aircraft were stored on the flight deck and five hundred cots were placed on the hanger deck. Only those of lofty rank were assigned to a stateroom bunk. All bunks and cots were on a "hot sack" basis. Two people were assigned to each for a different period of the day or night. When one's time was up, the next man would "sack out" for his allotted time.

Food was served twenty-four hours a day, which prevented a mile long chow line from stretching around the ship at meal times. Many a card game was played, many a loping domino was rolled, many a book was read and many a bull session was held, as we killed time on our long, slow journey across the Pacific. We counted the days until our arrival in the States.

We sailed into San Francisco Bay during the last week of October 1944. We were off-loaded to the Naval Air Station, Alameda, California. The air group reported to the Commander, Fleet Air Alameda. It was from Fleet Air Alameda, on 3 November 1944, that I received my orders that read, "*You are hereby detached from all duties, which may have been assigned you. You will proceed to Alameda, California and report to Commander Fleet Air Alameda, Naval Air Station, Alameda, California, for temporary duty, involving flying, in connection with reforming Fighting Squadron 31. You will continue on duty, involving flying, in that squadron, when reformed. You are authorized to delay a period of thirty days in reporting to your new duty station."*

I headed out right away and made the long, weary two thousand-mile journey back to Zavalla, Texas. During my thirty days of leave, I found a population that was firmly behind the war effort. Morale was high and they could not do enough for those in uniform. "Rosy the Riveter" had filled the shoes of those away in combat and rationing was being taken in stride. After all these years, I still remember a little ditty called "Duration Blues." It poked fun at the situation, and, at least for me, summed up the resolve of the home front.

"There's wham and spam and beveled ham and something there called zoom.
Just take it home and heat it to the temperature of the room.
You can make it, bake it, or take it anyway you choose.
That's the situation, it's called the Duration Blues."

My thirty days of leave went much too fast and before you knew it, the time had arrived to report to my duty station. I negotiated with the Ration Board and managed to procure enough gas ration chits and four tires for my car to make the return trip to Alameda, California.

On December 9, 1944, ten combat veterans returning from the old group formed the nucleus around which the new squadrons would be built. Forty-five other pilots, ranging from experienced fleet personnel to newly trained ensigns, rounded out the complement. After some initial training at Alameda, we moved south to Hollister, California, on January 7th. Hollister became our home base of operations, and we started our training in earnest.

I had added responsibility this time. As a combat veteran and an ace, I had been assigned as a division leader. I would be responsible for leading three other pilots through their training and into combat, a bit sobering.

Under the guidance of the combat experienced pilots the training went smoothly and swiftly. The squadrons became proficient in tactics, bombing, and aerial gunnery. We also had a few new skills to master. The Navy could now arm our planes with 5"rockets and we had to learn how to use them accurately.

There was also an increased emphasis on night flying and this cost us a valued friend. On 5 March, a four-plane division, led by our commanding officer conducting officer, Lt. Comdr. Daniel Wallace, was conducting routine night training over Monterey Bay. The flight director radioed him and ordered the flight to reverse course to avoid some bad weather in front of them. At 4,000 feet, Wallace led the flight into an easy right turn at a bank angle of 15°. Something happened – something went wrong. Wallace began to gain speed as his bank angle increased and he lost altitude. One section had to break off but his wingman stayed with Wallace, desperately calling to him on the radio. There was no answer and the wingman had to break off. Wallace's plane crashed into the ground. His death deeply shocked and saddened all of us. He was both liked and respected as a fine leader.

Commander Bruce S. Weber took command of the squadron and our training went on. Our preparation was intense but there were many moments of levity. I don't know what it is about a fighter pilot, but if there is a high bridge, he has to fly under it. This is against regulations and tends to annoy the powers that be. We had so many pilots flying under the San Francisco Bay

Angel In The Cockpit

Bridge that the local Naval Command assigned a duty airplane to circle over the bridge and record the tail numbers of any aircraft caught flying under it.

One day, just at dusk, I took my four-plane division under the bridge, in formation. I guess the duty airplane had secured for the day or could not see our numbers in the reduced light, since we were never called on the mat for it. Along with buzzing the bridges, we had our almost daily dogfights with the Army Air Corps. That not only gave us good training, but it also gave us a respite from our more tedious assignments.

Reforming and training the air group continued for four months. Finally, on 29 March 1945, we went aboard the *USS Monterey* for our return trip to the war zone. We sailed for Hawaii and our trip was uneventful except for the rolling and pitching of the ship in rough weather. That gave our new people a taste of sea life and seasickness. They were seldom seen out of their rooms, except when it was necessary to dash to the side railing for some relief, then back to their sacks.

The *Monterey* arrived at Pearl Harbor on 2 April 1945. Our air group flew off the ship before the entry into Pearl Harbor and was based at Barbers Point on the east side of the island of Oahu. To our dismay we learned another air group was to be assigned to the *Monterey*. This air group had been removed from a carrier hit by a Kamikaze and had trained in Hawaii while waiting for another deck to become vacant. VF-31 became the air group training in the Hawaiian Islands, waiting for an available carrier.

Let me tell you this, getting back into combat became a hard row to hoe. You would think all hands would be elated to be in Hawaii, miles from the combat zone with no one shooting at them. That was not the case. Every man was eager to get on with it and move to the front lines. We trained at Barbers Point for a while then transferred to Hilo, on the big island of Hawaii. Here we covered our full syllabus of training including gunnery, bombing, tactics, and night and day carrier landings. Our carrier landings were made on the *Monterey* and other available carriers in the area. During this period we had one mishap - two planes ran together in mid-air. One pilot was killed and the other was sent back to the States with a broken leg.

As I said, everyone was "chomping at the bit" to get back into combat. We were dedicated warriors, preparing ourselves for combat. But, being at this garden spot of the universe, not all actions were entirely serious. It was true that all the pilots had sharpened their skills in gunnery and bombing. It was also true that at least twenty pilots had lowered their handicaps on the nearby lush, green golf course.

There were also many moments of levity, which broke the tedious demands of training and the boredom of waiting for orders to move back to the combat zone. One such happening was a classic.

We had a Lieutenant Parker whom we lovingly called "Hog Jowls." Parker loved his beer and was a sound sleeper after a round of, say, six or eight brews. Late one evening, Parker, after having his regular ration of beer, left our festivities at the Officer's Club and retired to his room at the Bachelor Officer's Quarters (BOQ). After closing the bar, we returned to the BOQ and found Parker sound asleep in his room. Six of us gently picked up the mattress, with Parker on it, and moved it over to the other twin bed in the room. Then we tore down the bed and moved the frame and springs out to the middle of the parade ground next to the BOQ. We gently picked up the mattress, with Parker on it, took it out and placed it back on the bed frame and springs.

We turned in for the night, but we were all up at sunup to watch Parker's reaction when he woke. It was full daylight when Parker turned over once, then sat up with a start. He threw himself back on the pillow and pulled the covers up over his head. He stayed this way for about five minutes. Then he jumped up, wrapped the covers around himself and ran for the BOQ. We all gave him a rousing welcome as he entered the building. To this day, Parker maintains it was the best night's sleep he has ever experienced.

Our training at Hilo continued for a month and after extensive night carrier landing work, we flew to Ford Island in the middle of Pearl Harbor on Oahu. Pearl was a bustling place in 1945. Nearly all the damage from the Japanese raid three years earlier had been repaired. Sunken ships had been raised, repaired and returned to service. As we flew in, the only reminder of that attack we could see was the grim hulk of the battleship *Arizona*, still resting on the bottom of the harbor.

On Ford Island, we made preparation for going aboard the USS *White Plains*, to start our journey back into combat. This transfer and the loading of the air group aboard the *White Plains* took about four days. During this time the officers of the air group were housed at the BOQ on Ford Island.

As always when a ship comes into port and the air group is housed on shore, the big problem becomes scarcity of transportation. You could always check with the Motor Pool of the Command you are aboard and if a car or jeep was available, it could be checked out for use during the time you were there. Well, while we were at Ford Island we were lucky that the Motor Pool had a jeep. We were able to check it out and used it until the ship sailed.

We were elated with having the jeep to get us to different spots all over the island of Oahu. This elation turned to dismay when we returned to Ford Island one evening. It seemed that another squadron had come in to Ford Island. The Commanding Officer of the new squadron was senior to our Commanding Officer and he wanted the jeep. **R**ank **h**as **i**ts **p**rivileges, so we returned the jeep to the Motor Pool. For sure, this was not the end of the episode by a long shot. Our pilots had become a close knit unit since the re-commissioning of the air group and were not likely to let this little setback go unnoticed.

On the air group's last night on Ford Island before departing for combat once more, the festivities at the Officer's Club lasted well into the morning. It was at around 2:00 a.m. that about twenty-five of the air group's officers returned to the BOQ. Lo and behold, what was parked in front of the "Q" but our wayward jeep. It did not take long to devise a devious plan of attack and set it into motion. We dismantled the jeep as best we could. The twenty-five of us picked the jeep up, carried it up a flight of twelve steps, turned it on its side and squeezed it into the lobby of the BOQ. There we reassembled the jeep, placing it as if it was part of the furniture in the lobby. After a short nights sleep, we all reported aboard the *White Plains* early in the morning. We departed Pearl Harbor, secure in the knowledge that the officer who had taken our jeep was going to have a hard time explaining how the jeep got up twelve steps into the lobby of the BOQ. And who was going to get it out?

At last, we were on the *White Plains* heading to the combat zone. There we would go aboard the USS *Belleau Wood* as its assigned air group. Little did we know what a wild, leapfrog effort would be required to reach our assigned carrier. First, the *White Plains* dropped our air group on Saipan. Here we stayed for ten days. The only thing we accomplished during that time was to visit Isley Airfield, where the B-29 Bombers were flying day and night strike missions against the main island of Japan.

Angel In The Cockpit

On June 10th, the air group boarded the *USS Makassar Strait*, which took us to Guam, where we were to re-board the *USS White Plains*. This time the *White Plains* would take us to the *Belleau Wood*.

While in Guam, waiting to go aboard the *White Plains*, we were quartered in tents on the base. At this time, Guam still had many holdout Japanese solders in the woods and hills around the base. The Officer's Club was about two miles back in the woods from the main area of the base, and as usual, there was no local transportation.

Late one night, on our walk from the Officer's Club back to our tents, we had our first encounter with one of the Japanese who was hiding out near the base. We saw this person walking on the path ahead of us, and knowing it was safer to make the trip in numbers, we called to him to join us for our return to base. He turned, saw us and bolted into the woods, leaving us standing there in surprise. The next morning the base reported that the mess hall had been broken into the night before and some food had been taken. We assumed the Japanese solder we had seen was the culprit.

Our next encounter with one of the holdouts was a little scary. Four of us were billeted in one of the tents along with two Marine Corps Officers. About three o'clock in the morning, I awoke and saw a figure standing by one of the Marine Officers' bunks. He was going through a duffel bag. I raised up and shouted, "What are you doing there!" The man bolted for the door, dropping items as he ran. One of the items dropped was a 45-caliber pistol one of the Marine Corps Officers had laying close at hand. Needless to say, we slept with one eye open for the rest of the night.

Finally and happily, the next day we boarded the *USS White Plains* and sailed for Leyte Gulf in the Philippines. On the 16th of June 1945, we reported aboard as the assigned air group on the *USS Belleau Wood*. Repeating the words of General Douglas MacArthur when he went ashore with our amphibious forces on Leyte, I wrote in my flight log, "*I HAVE RETURNED!*"

USS *Belleau Wood* (CVL-24) was a familiar member of the Independence class of light carriers. She started life as the cruiser **New Haven** before being converted to an aircraft carrier. She entered service in 1943 and campaigned with Task Force 58 across the Pacific until severely damaged by a Kamikaze attack in late October of 1944. Repairs took four months.

Chapter Seven

The Philippines

After a shakedown in the last few days of June, Task Force 38 pulled out of Leyte Gulf and headed for the Japanese Homeland. The *Belleau Wood* was assigned to Task Group 38.1, along with three other carriers and many accompanying combat vessels. Task Force 38 was made up of four such task groups and our combat mission was to continue the softening-up of the Japanese mainland. This action called for the destruction of airfields, combat aircraft, shore batteries, all combat infrastructure and any remaining fleet combat ships. This preparation would culminate in an amphibious assault on the main island of Japan sometime in the near future.

On the trip north, we flew training missions to become familiar with fleet procedures. As we approached Japan, my division flew four combat air patrol missions over our task group. We received no opposition from the air or at sea as we moved within striking distance of our aircraft. It was as if the Japanese had pulled back their air and sea forces, to save all that they could to resist the amphibious assault that everyone knew was coming. It became our mission to maintain supremacy in the air over Japan while we sought out and destroyed any and all fighting equipment we could find on the ground.

Our combat operations began on 10 July 1945, when we launched fighter sweeps against Kumagaya Airfield in the Tokyo Plains area. My flight was assigned the destruction of aircraft located in revetments on and around the airfield. We made our initial pass and dropped our 500-pound bombs on the hangers and the installations near the airfield. It was obvious the Japanese were ready to make a maximum effort in the protection of their homeland when the amphibious assault began. They greeted us with the heaviest antiaircraft fire that I had ever encountered, heavier even than Task Force 58's defensive fire at Truk. As we made our attacks on the aircraft in the revetments, they would open up with intense fire from all sides of the airfield. The defenders also released helium filled balloons trailing steel cables, in hopes that we would fly into the cables and wreck our planes. Called barrage balloons by the British, these were new to us - just one more thing to worry about during an attack.

My flight was able to find six twin-engine aircraft in the revetments and burn or damage all six. I was able to get two burning and our bomb hits on the hangers had done major damage. My four planes returned to base without harm from the intense antiaircraft fire. The success of the overall mission was saddened by the loss of one of VF-31's fighter pilots from another division. On a strike in another area, he was reported to have taken a hit from the heavy antiaircraft fire that was being put up over the target. He crashed straight into the ground.

We continued attacks on targets in the Tokyo Plains area for the next three days, doing considerable damage to the airfields and the trains we found moving in the area. It was obvious that the Japanese were hoarding their combat aircraft for the expected invasion, since we experienced very intense antiaircraft fire from the ground but no resistance at all in the air.

Angel In The Cockpit

We then moved to the northernmost Japanese island of Hokkaido. We launched strikes and sweeps against inland airfields, port facilities, factories and rolling stock of all kinds. My flight was launched against the port of Rumoi on the western shore of Hokkaido. We made our attacks on ships in the harbor and left two merchant ships on fire and sinking. Then we turned our attention to locomotives in the area. We made repeated strafing attacks on fourteen different locomotives and left them in shambles. On our trip back across Hokkaido to our carrier, we made strafing attacks on an airfield, destroying twelve aircraft on the ground. We depleted what ordnance we had remaining on factory buildings that had been designated as targets. Again, we received no air-to-air resistance.

Bad weather and fog handicapped operations over and around Hokkaido. Returning from one strike, we found the fleet obscured in a thin layer of fog. The only portions of the fleet that could be seen were the masts that were sticking up through the fog. Knowing the formations of the ships we were able to pick out the mast belonging to our carrier. One by one we let down into the fog until the wake of the ship was visible. We then followed the wake until the landing signal officer was in view and followed his instructions to complete the landing. This tricky procedure was followed until all of our planes were back aboard.

After our strikes on Hokkaido, we returned to the Tokyo Plains area where we made a series of strikes on the old Japanese battleship *Nagato* docked at Yokosuka. We took heavy anti-aircraft fire from the docks nearby but little if any from the Nagato. We scored some hits with our bombs but the battleship was still afloat when we left.

The **Nagato** was one of the older Japanese battleships, launched in 1920. It served for a long time as the fleet flagship, until displaced by the massive **Yamato**. It was heavily damaged by air strikes during the battle of Leyte Gulf. At the time of Hawk's raid it was immobile due to lack of fuel and most of its anti-aircraft armament had been stripped for shore use. The Nagato survived the war to be sunk during the atomic bomb tests at Bikini Atoll in 1946.

These strikes on the *Nagato* were just a warm-up for what was to follow. Our next mission was the destruction of the fleet units based in Kure harbor. My flight of four was assigned the battleship *Ise* as our target. There was great excitement and considerable tension as we planed this mission. The antiaircraft fire at Kure was known to be very intense, with both shore batteries and fleet units firing. We expected the worst.

The IJN battleship **Ise** had a long and interesting career. Launched in 1917, she participated in the early battles of World War II such as the Pearl Harbor raid and Midway. In 1943, the *Ise* was converted to a hybrid aircraft carrier when her two rear turrets were removed and replaced with a flight deck. She was repeatedly used to ferry supplies and equipment to beleaguered Japanese strongholds such as Truk and Manila. She was never much of a success as an aircraft carrier and she was damaged in the Battle of Leyte Gulf. Immobilized by lack of fuel, she met her end at dockside in Kure harbor.

I sweated the launch because each of us was carrying a one thousand-pound armor-piercing bomb. An accident on takeoff would not only kill the pilot, but could kill many of the *Belleau Wood* crew. Fortunately, we took off without incident, then climbed to 20,000 feet and joined the other aircraft on the strike.

Angel In The Cockpit

Shortly after we reached altitude, Dickey Lawler, the number four man of my division started acting crazy. He streaked away from the formation, then turned and came back for us, almost as if he were in an attack mode.

"Dickey, what are you doing?" one of the other men in my division asked.

We were supposed to be under radio silence, and the pilot who broke the silence concerned me as much as Dickey's erratic flying. Putting my thumb on the "transmit" button, I broke squelch twice. This sent two "pops" into the headsets of the other pilots and, in so doing, reiterated the need for radio silence.

By now, Dickey was coming toward us for the second time and, just as he reached us, he peeled up to climb over us. At the same time, I saw the thousand-pound bomb leave his aircraft and fall through the formation, passing so close a'port that I could read the message the armorer had chalked on it as he loaded it.

YOU ARE GOING TO GET A BANG OUT OF THIS ONE

I held my breath as the bomb passed through without hitting anyone. I realized then that something was going to have to be done – and fast - before Dickey killed us all.

By hand signals, I turned the lead of my flight over to my section leader. Then I joined as tight as I could on Dickey's wing. That was when I saw the problem. Dickey had not put on his oxygen mask and was now suffering from a bad case of anoxia. Technically, when one is drunk, it is because alcohol causes the brain to suffer oxygen deprivation. Though Dickey had not had a drink, he was drunk!

I took my own oxygen mask off and shook it at him. At first, he thought I was just waving at him, and, with a big smile, he waved back. I made a big show of putting my mask on, then taking it off, and putting it on again. After about three attempts at this, he finally understood what I was saying to him. He nodded at me, then fumbled around for his mask and put it on. After a few breaths of 100% oxygen, he settled down and rejoined the division.

With my division now intact, we approached the target, beginning a slow descent until we reached ten thousand feet. I pointed out our target, the battleship *Ise,* and the others in the division wagged their wings in recognition. Immediately, black puffs of antiaircraft shells filled the sky as the Japanese gunners tried to zero in on our altitude.

As the leader, I was the first to fall off into a dive, followed closely by the other three aircraft of my division. For the first few seconds of the dive, the black puffs of air-burst shells stayed with me. But as the dive continued, the AA guns were no longer able to track. I wasn't out of the woods though, because the deadly flowers disappeared, only to be replaced by streaks of tracers coming from smaller guns that had picked up our planes. I dove from the stern to the bow of the *Ise* and held the piper of my gun sight directly on the bow of the ship. At eighteen hundred feet I released my bomb, pulled up and did a right turn on my escape route. From this turn I was able to see my bomb hit just forward of the *Ise's* bridge structure.

Once I regained altitude, I twisted around in my seat just in time to see a torpedo bomber that had been making an antiaircraft suppression attack on ground targets explode. It had taken a direct hit from an antiaircraft shell, and as pieces of the aircraft settled to the water, I saw no parachutes to indicate that anyone had survived.

I returned to the carrier with my division and the post-flight photographs showed that the *Ise* had sunk and was resting on the bottom of the harbor. We were elated that the mission had been a success. But this elation was more than offset when we learned that we had lost one of our squadron's torpedo bombers with a crew of three. We weren't the only squadron to lose a torpedo bomber on that raid, so there was no way of knowing if the aircraft I had seen take the hit from the antiaircraft fire was the one from our own air group.

The week following the 24 July Kure harbor attacks, we continued strikes in the Nagoya area, laying to waste factories and other combat infrastructure. Fifteen Japanese fighters jumped one of our strikes, in our first sign of any air-to-air resistance since returning to combat. I was not on this flight but our fighters did themselves proud in knocking down eight of the attackers, however, we did lose two pilots in this engagement. We did not know it at the time, but one of the pilots survived his shoot down to be taken prisoner.

As our air strikes continued daily in the Nagoya area, my flight of four was a part of a strike on the Kagamigahara airfield. Upon arriving at the target we released our bombs on the runways and revetments around the airfield. It turned out to be a rather rich target, because the Japanese had aircraft sitting on the taxi ramps, fully fueled and ready for flight. As the tracers from our 50 caliber guns struck the fueled aircraft, they would burst into flames. After our attack, twenty-two enemy aircraft were left burning and black smoke almost obscured the airfield. Although the antiaircraft fire was extremely heavy, all of my flight returned safely.

We learned later that these airplanes were to have been used in the Japanese final suicide attacks against our invasion fleet.

As it turned out though, fortunately for the thousands of army and marine troops who would have been used, the invasion never took place. That was because, on the 6th of August, a B-29, the Enola Gay, dropped a single atomic bomb on Hiroshima destroying the city. Three days later, a second atomic bomb was dropped, leveling the city of Nagasaki.

After these events, the Japanese accepted the Potsdam Ultimatum, but with reservations. The fighting continued through the next five days since the reservations added by the Japanese were not unconditional surrender, as agreed upon at the Potsdam Conference. The war would not be over until the unconditional surrender was accepted.

My four-plane flight was part of a major strike each of the five days. We hit the heavily defended electronic industry just twelve miles to the south of Tokyo. We struck Osaka, Sendi and Matsuyama factories leaving them in flames from our bombs and gunfire. On one strike my four planes hit Tsukuba West airfield and found many aircraft on the line being readied for take off. Our repeated attacks left twenty-five aircraft burning and debris scattered from the force of their detonating fuel tanks. We figured these planes were Kamikazies being prepared for a final strike on our fleet, where they could die gloriously for their emperor.

On the fifth day of these attacks, 15 August 1945, at four o'clock in the morning we launched a fighter sweep of the Tokyo Plains area. As they reached the coast, six enemy fighters attacked the flight. During the ensuing dogfight all six enemy planes were shot down. My flight was launched about thirty minutes behind this sweep - we were to bomb assigned targets in the Tokyo area. We were each carrying a 1,000-pound bomb. Word came over the radio, from the Admiral of the Fleet: Japan had accepted the unconditional surrender - the war was over!

We were directed to drop the bombs in the water and return to base. We jettisoned our bombs and every pilot excitedly broke radio silence. There were shouts of, "It's over; let's all go home!" "Hurrah! I made it; tell Mama I'm coming home!"

"Tojo, you asked for it, and baby you got it!" Somewhere in there, the old battle-cry, "Remember Pearl Harbor!" was heard. Radio discipline became so bad, with all this jubilation going on, that the radio became nothing but a big noise. Using the old CB slang, "Everybody was getting stepped on by everybody else." Something had to be done to clear the airways so that normal operations could proceed. Cooler heads prevailed, the jubilation subsided somewhat, and everybody got headed back to the fleet for landing.

As we headed back to base, radar noted a lot of air action going on over the beach as all kinds of aircraft were taking off and heading out toward the fleet. The Admiral could not know whether these planes were just some curious observers or were Kamikaze pilots, on their way out to give up their lives in a suicide dive into one of our ships. He ordered any enemy aircraft that did not heed the warning to steer clear of the fleet, to be shot down in a "friendly fashion." As the day wore on some six enemy aircraft that failed to heed the warning to stay clear, met this "friendly" fate.

We were kept informed of the jubilation, taking place back in the States and throughout the Allied world, as word of the Japanese surrender became known. Certainly, we in the combat zone shared in that jubilation. However, along with the jubilation, our flight requirements were not reduced. There was much to be done as preparations got underway for the formal signing of the peace treaty.

Chapter Eight

Peace Treaty

With the unconditional surrender of the Japan, we thought that things would ease up, but they didn't. A lot of planning was underway to insure that the official signing of the peace treaty was done in a manner that would bring credit to the victors. The war that had been forced upon the United States by the unprovoked Japanese attack on Pearl Harbor, was coming to a close and the occupation of Japanese Islands was before us. Acceptance of the surrender, the planning for the signing of the peace treaty and the occupation fell under the overall joint command of General Douglas Mac Arthur as Commander of the Southeast Asia Command and Admiral Chester Nimitz, Commander in Chief, Pacific Fleet.

The first order of business was the naval occupation of the Tokyo area. By Pacific Fleet communiqué, Admiral William F. Halsey, Commander U.S. Third Fleet was put in charge of the project. His was not an easy task as the naval forces scheduled to enter the Japanese waters in the first stage of the occupation were massive. The force included the Admiral's flag ship, the battleship *USS Missouri* and several hundred other ships, from carriers to freighters.

I was stunned to see the size of this massive force. I realized that it, and all the other machines of war required to fight two wars, were produced by the people of the United States in less than four years following December 7th, 1941. It made me feel that, when our freedom is threatened, good old Yankee ingenuity will find no task impossible.

Many meetings were held with representatives of Japan to establish ground rules to be followed, leading up to the signing of the peace treaty. No-fly zones, disabling of all shore batteries and the clear markings of all POW camps in Japan were but a few of the rules. The policing of these ground rules became the task of the aircraft from Task Force 38.

My division, along with others, flew combat air patrols over the no-fly zones to insure no aircraft entered the area. We flew interdiction flights along all the coastlines, checking on the shore batteries. If we found any with the weapons still pointing toward the sea we made dry runs on the gun position until the weapon orientation was corrected. If there was no movement of the weapon we were to "take military action" to ensure compliance. Let me tell you there were some Japanese gun crews that learned to move pretty fast when our .50 caliber shells started hitting around their gun position.

The flights that gave us the most satisfaction were the POW flights. The Japanese were directed to paint large white letters of POW on the top of the buildings of each POW camp. Our flights would spread out over Japan and, when we located a camp, our bomber aircraft would be directed in to drop food, clothing, and any items we felt the prisoners could use. I will detail one of the flights and its results in the following chapter.

We continued flying interdiction, combat air patrol and POW missions from the day of unconditional surrender, August 25th, until the day scheduled for the official signing of the peace treaty.

Angel In The Cockpit

On the 2nd of September everything was ready, down to the last detail, for the official signing. The battleship *USS Missouri*, where the ceremony was to be held, was decked out splendidly. All senior officials of the Allied Powers were on board to observe the signing. One of the lesser details that had been orchestrated by General Mac Arthur was to insure that every Military Policeman who was to form the escort for the Japanese Officials as they boarded the Missouri for the signing, be six feet in height or taller. This was obviously to make the Japanese, who were smaller in frame, feel inferior.

General Mac Arthur had also directed that as many aircraft as could be put in the air should fly over the Missouri at the moment of signing. My division of four was a part of more than a thousand aircraft launched from the sixteen carriers of Task Force 38 for this massive fly-over. The flight was put under an in-flight commander. All planes were launched, the rendezvous completed and a wide orbit was started to put us over the *Missouri* at the time of signing. As any aviator will tell you, when you have a thousand aircraft in one flight, all turns, climbs or let downs must be made as gently as possible. This being the case things did not go too smoothly.

The weather was not the greatest. We had a low broken overcast at around 2,000 to 2,500 ft. With a thousand aircraft stacked down in formation under this overcast, someone had to be dragging very close to the water. There were a bunch of unhappy aviators as the flight drug on. Radio discipline became unbearable as shouts of, "lets get this show on the road" and other words of unrepeatable wisdom filled the airways.

Finally word came to head in toward the Missouri as the signing was taking place. Things looked pretty good as the formation was somewhat in tact and on schedule to arrive over the *Missouri* at the proper time. That was, until a flight of twenty to thirty B-29's out of Iwo Jima was observed closing on the *Missouri* from the opposite direction. Believe me, those required gentle turns I described earlier immediately became very violent. The good Lord must have been with us as everyone made it through safe and sound. General Mac Arthur certainly got his wish to have planes overhead as a show of power while the Japanese signed the surrender. The sky was black with planes going in all directions. We all returned safely to our carriers, the Peace Treaty was signed and the war was officially over.

Chapter Nine

Prisoner of War Flights

In the preceding chapter I mentioned a special prisoner of war flight that I flew. It ended with such a pleasing outcome that I wanted to devote an entire chapter to it. The following is what happened on that flight and afterwards.

With the surrender of Japan, a high priority task for the naval aviation forces in the Pacific was making contact with the thousands of Allied prisoners of war throughout Japan. The specific assignment was to locate the prisoner of war camps and quickly deliver food, clothing, medical supplies and hope to the men who had endured the ordeal of Japanese imprisonment. The tools available were the combined resources of naval aviation in the area and information and instructions that came out of the initial meeting between the Allies and Japan following the surrender. From this meeting, the Japanese had agreed to paint the large letters "PW" on the rooftops of buildings in each camp. They also gave a general location of each camp. The POW's were free from Japanese oppression, but they still did not have adequate food, clothing and other supplies. Our orders were to fly over Japan, locate the camps and make drops of food, clothing and medical supplies. Flying from the *Belleau Wood,* I made four such flights in search of the camps. I will relate what happened on one special flight and its outcome that spanned more than forty years.

On the morning of 22 August 1945, I took off from the *Belleau Wood* with my division of fighters and we headed for Japan. Our mission was to locate POW camps in the northwestern part of Honshu, the main island of Japan. Once a camp was located, I was to call in our bomber aircraft that were orbiting well to the east. The bombers were loaded with foods medical supplies and clothing to be dropped into the camp compounds for the prisoners. We arrived over the general area about midday near Naoetsu, in the mountainous northwest part of Honshu. All morning we had been flying through threatening weather. We found the area nearly covered by clouds with a light snow falling. I left the other members of my division orbiting in the clear and went down below the overcast to take a look. I found what we had been briefed to look for. There were lines of buildings with large white "PW's" painted on the roofs. I had found the prison of hundreds of American, British, Dutch and Australian POW's.

I made several passes over the camp and was greeted by wildly waving men. I realized that there was little point in trying to bring the bombers through the worsening weather. I dug out my message drop kit, and penciled a brief note of explanation that the weather would prevent our bombers from getting through. The note assured them that we would be back tomorrow with food and supplies. I dropped the note and made one more pass to make sure the note was received. I watched as a man picked up the note near the camp. I rejoined my flight above the overcast and we returned to the *Belleau Wood*.

We did return with the bombers the following day. Load after load of food, boots, medicine, clothing and cigarettes were dropped beside and on the flimsy buildings throughout the day.

We continued the drops for two more days until we were met by messages on the rooftops of the camp, "Enough please. No More. Thanks. Any News?"

This was my last POW flight. Our attention returned to giving coverage to the battleship *Missouri* and other ships as they came into anchor in preparation for the signing of the surrender by Japan.

Orange Beach, Alabama: Today

As I said in the first chapter, the beauty of memory is that it allows you to recall events, out of sequence, if you wish. And, as I sat here working on these memoirs, something that happened much more recently popped into my mind.

In early March of 1986, I received a bulky envelope that was postmarked from New South Wales, Australia, and addressed to LIEUTENANT Ray Hawkins.

Now, since I had no known family, acquaintances, or contacts in Australia, and since it had been over forty years since I was a lieutenant, you can imagine my curiosity as I opened the package to see what it was.

As soon as I looked inside, though, I was transported back to another time and place, awakening long dormant memories of a snowy day over the mountains of northern Japan in August of 1945.

The envelope contained a letter from a Mr. Matt Clift, a past member of the Australian Imperial Army, 2nd Infantry Division 20th Battalion, who had been captured by the Japanese in the fall of Singapore. He had been interned in the Naoetsu POW Camp. Although I didn't know it at the time, he was the one I watched picking up THE message I dropped back in August of 1945. I will share with you his letter:

Dear Lieutenant Hawkins:

I should have written you some 40 years ago after I had returned from that hellhole POW camp at Naoetsu, situated on the northwest corner of Honshu Island and 53 hours by train from Nagasaki. Along with us Aussies, in Naoetsu, were servicemen from the Dutch East Indies, British, and Americans. Of the 300 Australian POW's who arrived at Naoetsu on 12 October 1942, from Changi POW Camp in Singapore, only 240 survived. The others died because they were either kicked to death, starved deliberately to death, or tortured to death by the sadistic Japanese guards.

On 15 August, we were told by the Japs that the war was over. However, they stated that they would still stand guard over us as a precaution against any possible threat that the Japanese civilians might be contemplating against us. We were all recalled to camp from the foundries, at the stainless steel works, where we were usually employed at this particular period. From then on, bashings and all forms of harassment by the Japanese eased and we were much more or less left to our own devices. Of course the quality of the food rationed to us was small, tasteless, and of doubtful nutritional value.

On 20 August, I strolled down to the bank of the deep, fast flowing river that bordered our camp, where I sat down with my thoughts. I looked up to the sky above with its heavy overcast and whitish gray snow clouds that were menacingly low. Suddenly, I heard the drone of an aeroplane overhead. I looked up and your plane came into view through a very slight break in the cloud cover. I watched as your plane circled and when you were almost immediately above me, I noticed something drop from the plane. I could see that whatever it was, it was heading directly into the fast flowing river. That is where it certainly would have ended up had I not leaned out over the river, with my body and arms extended to their absolute extreme, and I thought that it was certain that I would end up in the icy cold drink. Suddenly (I really don't know how) I was standing erect on the river bank with the object, with the yellow flowing tail, securely in my hands. It's funny, almost pathologically stupid, what starving people do and think. These are my own, truthful reactions as I handled this strange object dropped from the sky. My first thought was, "This is a block of hard chocolate". Then I thought what a great bloke that Yank pilot must be to drop a bar of chocolate just for me. I struggled with the object, wrenching back and forth, twisting it this way and that way. No go. (Come to think of it now, I wonder if you even noticed me?)

You can imagine my disappointment (suffering from starvation) to find that the object was not edible, but a piece of wood covered with material into which a slot was cut to hold messages dropped from planes. Attached was a yellow material tail about 2'6" long and about 4" wide. My initial assessment of you as a damn good bloke dwindled somewhat. I withdrew the penciled message and handed both the message and container to my Australian Commander, Captain Chisholm (since deceased). He read the note which stated that because of the bad weather it would be tomorrow before planes would be in to drop food and stuff.

The planes arrived and when the first drop occurred (there being but little space in the small camp rooms) all men were requested to come forward and be issued with six packets of cigarettes each. Such was the inadequacy of storage space, that the officers were calling almost continuously for the men to come forward, and we were all eventually overloaded with cartons upon cartons of every available brand of cigarettes, chocolates, K-rations etc. Verily enough of everything that we had been starved of for years.

Many loads fell outside the camp perimeter, some (miraculously) were returned to us by the Japs who retrieved them, but naturally many were not returned. We just couldn't care less, with everyone of us talking, smoking, and stoking up with chocolate, k-rations, etc. We were, for that day, in heaven.

Alas!! There is always a tomorrow and of course, on this occasion, the tomorrow asked its price and we paid. The next day, August 22, practically the entire camp complement was afflicted with the severest diarrhea. Queues lining up in lavatories and in some cases (unable to hold on) evacuating wherever suitable space available. This, of course, resulted from our change of diet. Fortunately, the diarrhea soon cleared up and we were all fit and well again, with the exception of a mate of mine, Frank Hole, who suffered a broken leg when struck by a container which broke away from its parachute and struck him down.

From here on in everything was downhill and enjoyable until we, at long last, boarded the train at Naoetsu Station on the first stage of our journey home.

Some 25 years ago I considered trying to contact you, but when I became aware of the fact that I had no idea of where you may be living, and the thought of all the hassle and time that could be involved in tracing your whereabouts, I just gave the whole idea away.

Then, in 1983, Colonel and Mrs. Bob Pebles, USMC, who had years earlier hosted Miss Christine Carr of Australia as an exchange student, contacted Miss Carr's father in Sydney, New South Wales (he is a relation of mine by marriage) to say that they were coming to Australia in October, 1985. While the Pebles were visiting Cowra, I got to meet them. I showed Bob (a retired Marine Colonel naval aviator) your message packet and its message. He assured me that when he returned to the United States he would somehow find your address and forward it to me. This is precisely what he did. So now you know how I found the needle in the haystack.

I enclose herewith a photostat copy of your own original message. It was a great and momentous message of hope for all of us, and I know that you must be a fair dinkum bloke.

Very best regards,
Matt Clift

I corresponded with Matt over the years and he was kind enough to donate the original kit and message that was dropped into the camp. The two items are prominently displayed in the National Museum of Naval Aviation in Pensacola, Florida. From Matt's letters I learned a lot about him and his treatment in the POW camp.

After the fall of France, Matt volunteered for infantry service in the Australian Imperial Army at the age of 38. His Infantry Battalion was an entirely volunteer force. After training, his Infantry Division was assigned duty in Singapore and his

Battalion was assigned to the eastern coast of Malaya, in the Mersing River area.

The following is Matt's recollections of events:

"We established a very formidable defense around Mersing to guard against any sea borne attack. I fought in Malaya and Singapore, until Singapore was surrendered by the British. We were told to lay down our arms and await the arrival of the Japanese army.

"Shortly thereafter, we were marched to Changi Jail, very tired, disillusioned and furious at the decision to capitulate. Much later we were loaded aboard the Kamakura Maru, a modern 17,000-ton passenger cargo vessel, for the trip to Japan.

"Our food on the ship was poor, only two meals a day, usually a little rice and a thin stew. We were packed like sardines on the open "A" deck.

"On December 4, 1942, as we neared Japan, it got very cold on deck. We were used to the tropics, so the bitter cold and wind was hard to take in our thin khakis.

"We arrived in Nagasaki on December 8th, one year exactly after the Japanese entered the war.

"We left the ship alphabetically. Our group became a party of 300, up to the letter "S", and then we were marched to the railroad station. There, we were given Russian overcoats with fur collars, left over from the Russo-Japanese War of 1905.

"That same afternoon, we boarded a train (fortunately heated) for the 52 hour ride to Naoetsu, our POW site, located on the west coast of Japan. Snow was falling as we were loaded into trucks and driven to an old school.

Angel In The Cockpit

We slept on grass mats, extremely crowded together, which was to our advantage because of the cold.

"As prisoners, the 300 of us were put to work in one of three places, a stainless steel factory, or on barges loading and unloading or, as in my case, in a Mitsubishi steel plant. This plant manufactured carbide metal silicone in large dry cell electrodes. There were a number of these furnaces which were kept operating 24 hours a day.

"My job for nearly the whole time of my imprisonment was shoveling heavy metal into large wooden boxes. When filled, another POW and I would push them up a steep ramp and dump their contents into one of the furnaces. This would go on all day every day.

"Early in my imprisonment, for some obscure reason, our Jap interpreter ordered me to be in charge of a party of twenty-five
 POWs. We were supposed to learn some of their lingo so we could understand their orders.

"So he took my group to a small room where he had a blackboard and on it he wrote Jap numbers and their equivalent in English: (1) "itch" (2) "nee" (3) "san," etc. He then told me I had 30 minutes to teach the others the Japanese numbers.

"In retrospect, I must have been as big an idiot as I considered him to be. I just lined the men up in a straight line and told them to remember one number only. After a few practices of "itch," "nee," "san" and "see," I felt our training was going fine.

"When the Nip returned, he shouted out "say-ton" (which we later learned meant, put everything in order). But when he yelled "say-ton" we all sat down. After he had booted us around for awhile, he began shouting "boon-go," We finally realized he wanted us to line up and fall-in, which we did.

Then he showed us how to "ky-ree (bow)."

Then he ordered me to "number off." So I yelled "From the right, boon-go." There was complete silence. So he began kicking us again, particularly me. Needless to say, we finally learned enough Japanese to get by.

"I was only one among many, and I can only say this, no word has ever been coined, nor has language ever been constructed by which it would be possible to convey the trauma, physical, mental and spiritual, or the frustration, torture, starvation and brutality which was inflicted on us. It is also impossible for me to convey the courage, pride, comradeship and determination of the POWs, to maintain their dignity in the face of such brutality".

Matt and his countrymen would suffer for a hard three and a half years until their release in August 1945. Of the three hundred who were interned in the Naoetsu POW camp, sixty would not survive. Even after forty-two years, Matt's bitterness toward his captors never diminished.

Matt and I stayed in touch, and in one letter he sent along a poem that was written by one of his comrades in the Naoetsu POW camp. This poem of thanks to the pilots who flew the rescue missions over the camps, is at the end of this chapter.

Matt often talked of his desire to visit the United States, and we spoke of such things as a reunion at the National Museum of Naval Aviation, where the message and kit were on display. Alas, this was not to be, It was with deep sadness that I received a letter from a niece of Matt's, telling me that Matt had passed away. He would not be making the trip he so looked forward to. With Matt's death, this "fair dinkum bloke" had lost a good friend who will be sorely missed. I never had the chance to tell Matt, or found out if he already knew, that the Australian and American War Crimes Commission sentenced twelve prison guards of Naoetsu to death and several others to long prison terms.

POEM TO THE U.S NAVY PILOTS AND CREWS
WHO RESCUED THE WORLD WAR II POWs

by J. Nicholls, 2/20th Btn., Australian Imperial Forces

Our moment has come, after long weary years,
We watch speeding planes, our eyes wet with tears,

Just a mad cheering crowd as you go winging by,
A real message of hope from out of the sky,

We know it's the end of this living hell,
You've brought us a message we realize well.

Home again with our dear ones to the country we love,
A dream realized by your message above,

So God speed you boys as you wing on your way,
We thank you again and all wish to say

We'll never forget you as years roll away,
May you have all the joy you've brought us today.

— Nicco

Chapter Ten

Civilian

After the signing we had not received an operational plan, but it was obvious that the air group would be employed for a time flying protection over our occupation forces. This was not to be the case for me, as the "powers to be" had put out qualifications for those who could be returned to the States immediately, discharged and allowed to returned to their homes. These qualifications evaluated such things as to the length of time served in combat, combat missions flown, combat decorations received and a host of such other qualifications.

Under these guidelines, two other pilots and I were selected from the Fighter Squadron and were told to pack our bags. We would be leaving for the states immediately. It was clear that demobilization had begun.

On 6 September 1945 we were sent to the Ulithi Anchorage. We reported into the center that had been set up to furnish transportation for this first wave of people to be returned stateside. The center, we found, was the focus of mass confusion. They had no advance warning and no time to get organized before the first wave of people released for immediate return, descended upon them. After ten days at the center, it seemed that it would probably be weeks before transportation became available.

We three pilots and three other officers from our ship decided we would try to speed up the process. We were able to commandeer a small boat and began making the rounds of the more than fifty merchant ships anchored in Ulithi.

We made stops at about fifteen ships asking them if they were returning to the states. Things were not looking very good until we contacted the *SS Lyon's Creek*. *We were told* they would be leaving the next day for Balboa, Canal Zone. We asked the Master if he had space for six officers who were trying to get back to the States. He said he had six beds in his small unused hospital that he would be happy for us to use. Panama was not actually where we wanted to go but at least it was in the right direction. It would get us out of the mass of humanity that was building up at the center. We happily accepted and told him we would be back with our gear in a couple of hours - ready to depart in the morning.

As we went about getting our gear together, there was one little problem we had to work out - how we were going to get our original orders and have them endorsed by the center for travel on the *SS Lyon's Creek*. We looked up the leading yeoman of the center and told him what we had found space on a merchant ship that was leaving for the States the next day. We asked him if he could come up with our original orders. He allowed as how it would not be easy and he was not sure if we would be allowed to leave on a merchant ship. Somehow he came up with the proper papers with a typed endorsement directing us to proceed to the States on transportation as assigned. I'm sure that the Transportation Center eventually wondered, "What ever happened to those six officers that came in from the *Belleau Wood?"*

With us safely aboard the *SS Lyon's Creek* we departed for the Canal Zone. We quickly found out that the top speed of the

Lyon's Creek was ten knots, so we knew we were in for a long boring trip. Knowing the war was over and we were on our way home, we did not let the boredom bother us and thirty long days later we anchored at Bolboa, Canal Zone.

We immediately found out that we had hit another delay. All merchant ships had to stay in quarantine for several days. I asked the Master to send a message to the Admiral in charge of the Navy Command in the Canal Zone that six Naval officers were aboard and were requesting permission to come ashore.

Well let me tell you this message stirred up hornets' nest. Blinker messages started to flow in rapid session between our ship and the Naval Command ashore. They wanted to know who we were, where the ship had picked us up and what aviation or ship command we were from? The Navy Command first thought that the *Lyon's Creek* had picked us up out of the water following an aircraft crash or a ship sinking. After they were told we were Naval Officers being transported to the States for discharge, things cooled down and the Admiral's barge came out and picked us up.

We reported to the 15th Naval District in Balboa, C.Z, and they assigned us to another Transportation Center for further transfer to the States. During our thirty day crossing these centers had become a little more organized as they were all under one big operation called "Magic Carpet." We could see right off that, with the mass of people they had for transfer, our stay at the center was not to be a short one. Being old hands at the game, we managed to hold on to our original orders and started searching for transportation on our own.

While having a beer at the Officers Club, three of us met a pilot who was flying a big old PBM flying boat up to Miami the following morning. He told us that he had room and we were welcome to come along for the ride. We were on our way again and I wouldn't be surprised if *that* center wondered what happened to the three Naval Officers who reported in for transportation, but never left.

The **PBM** was a large "flying boat" built by Martin Aviation. It had two engines, a range of more than two thousand miles and a crew of up to eight men. It served throughout the war as a transport and long range scout, as well as anti-submarine patrols.

Arriving in Miami we reported into the Naval District Headquarters. Members of the Headquarters Staff had a hard time comprehending how we had left the *Belleau Wood* in Tokyo Bay and ended up in Miami on the East Coast of the United States. I think they must have assumed we really did have a "Magic Carpet". Be that as it may, they followed Navy directives and sent us to the military base closest to our home of record, where we would be discharged. I was sent to Camp Wallace, Texas, where I was processed and discharged from the Navy. For me the war had come to a successful conclusion and I was once again a civilian.

PHOTO ALBUM FROM WORLD WAR II

VF-31, The Early Days

Top Row L-R: Bowie, Hayde, Anderson, Loomis
Third Row L-R: Scales, Wirth, Hendrick, Zimmerman, Charity
Second Row L-R: Wilson, Hawkins, Nooy, Galt, Carr
First Row L-R: Winston, Patterson, Mencin, Kona, Jamison

Division Six: Hawk is top row center

Christmas of 1943. That's me just right of center front(singing). No liquor on board ship, we were drinking fruit punch.

Angel In The Cockpit

Above is me in my Hellcat, complete with flags to denote the air to air kills, and bombs marking the ground attack missions.

Following pages are citations for Distinguished Flying Crosses and Air Medals

Admiral Marc Mitscher. He won a permanent spot in the hearts of all the pilots the night he lit up the carriers . . . despite the threat of attack by Japanese planes . . . in order to facilitate our own return.

I am receiving my first DFC, or Distinguished Flying Cross.

I am "Home again, home again, home is the sailor from the sea."

In the name of the President of the United States, the Commander, Fast Carrier Task Forces, United States Pacific Fleet, presents the DISTINGUISHED FLYING CROSS to

LIEUTENANT (JG) ARTHUR R. HAWKINS
UNITED STATES NAVAL RESERVE

for service as set forth in the following

CITATION:

"For extraordinary achievement in action while his task force was under attack by low-flying enemy planes near TRUK. He was catapulted in the midst of heavy anti-aircraft fire directed at an enemy torpedo-bomber in the center of his task group. With complete disregard for his own safety he courageously pursued the enemy plane as it went past his base carrier following it through the heavy volume of fire and shooting it down in flames. This daring and successful action was distinguished by the precision of its execution and was in every respect in keeping with the highest traditions of the naval service."

M. A. MITSCHER,
Vice Admiral, U. S. Navy.

Temporary Citation.

In the name of the President of the United States, the Commander, FIRST Carrier Task Force, United States Pacific Fleet, presents the GOLD STAR in lieu of a second DISTINGUISHED FLYING CROSS to

LIEUTENANT (JUNIOR GRADE) ARTHUR RAY HAWKINS
UNITED STATES NAVAL RESERVE

for service as set forth in the following

CITATION:

"For heroic and extraordinary achievement in the line of his profession while participating in aerial flight under fire. On 19 June 1944, during the invasion of the Marianas, he was a member of a twelve-plane fighter group flying combat air patrol over the task group when they were vectored out about 50 miles to intercept a large enemy bogey of at least 30 fighters. In the face of these heavy odds and with complete disregard for his own safety he courageously attacked the enemy formation shooting down three planes, all of which were seen to crash into the sea. The six planes from his carrier accounted for a total of 15 planes shot down in this engagement. His skill and courage contributed greatly to the success of this engagement and were in keeping with the highest traditions of the naval service."

M. A. MITSCHER,
Vice Admiral, U. S. Navy.

Temporary Citation.

UNITED STATES PACIFIC FLEET
COMMANDER CARRIER DIVISION THREE

In the name of the President of the United States, the Commander Carrier Division THREE, Pacific, takes pleasure in presenting the GOLD STAR in lieu of a third DISTINGUISHED FLYING CROSS to

LIEUTENANT (JUNIOR GRADE) ARTHUR RAY HAWKINS
UNITED STATES NAVAL RESERVE

for service as set forth in the following

CITATION:

"For extraordinary achievement while participating in aerial flight as pilot of a United States Navy carrier based fighter plane in operations against the enemy on 13 August 1945. In a fighter strike against enemy airfields in the vicinity of Tokyo, Japan, he and his flight ignored medium and accurate anti-aircraft fire to aggressively carry out low level attacks on heavily camouflaged planes at four different airfields, destroying an impressive total of twenty-two planes and damaging twenty others on the ground. He continued strafing until forced to return because of exceedingly low gasoline supply. His aggressiveness and daring were at all times in keeping with the highest traditions of the United States Naval Service."

T. L. SPRAGUE,
Rear Admiral, U. S. Navy

Angel In The Cockpit

UNITED STATES PACIFIC FLEET
COMMANDER SEVENTH FLEET

In the name of the President of the United States the Commander SEVENTH FLEET, takes pleasure in presenting the Gold Star in lieu of the

DISTINGUISHED FLYING CROSS, (Fourth Award) to

Lieutenant Arthur R. HAWKINS, 240469/1310, U. S. Navy
Fighter Squadron ONE HUNDRED NINETY ONE
In the Korean Theater

on 10 February 1951

Basis of award: For heroism and extraordinary achievement in aerial flight as Pilot of a Jet Fighter Plane in Fighter Squadron ONE HUNDRED NINETY ONE, attached to the U.S.S. PRINCETON, (CV-37), in action against enemy forces in Central Korea, on 10 February 1951. Launched from his carrier as the leader of a two plane flight to sweep an important enemy supply route leading from Ch'unch' on north through Seoul, Lieutenant HAWKINS courageously led his flight into repeated low level rocket and strafing attacks through a blinding snow storm that covered the entire assigned route. As a result of these daring attacks three (3) locomotives and one (1) enemy T-34 tank were left a mass of destruction. By his heroic leadership, fighting spirit and devotion to duty in this engagement he upheld the highest traditions of the United States Naval Service.

H. M. MARTIN,
Vice Admiral, U. S. Navy
Commander SEVENTH Fleet

In the name of the President of the United States, the Commander, Fast Carrier Task Forces, United States Pacific Fleet, presents the AIR MEDAL to

Lieutenant (junior grade) Arthur Ray Hawkins
United States Naval Reserve

for service as set forth in the following

CITATION

For distinguishing himself by meritorious achievement while participating in aerial flight as the pilot of a single seater carrier based fighter plane. On 8 July 1944 while flying Combat Air Patrol over his Task Group his four-plane division was vectored out about thirty miles to assist a division of fighters who were engaged in an air battle with a group of enemy planes. He courageously entered the fight and, in a headon attack, shot down one enemy plane while his division accounted for a total of three planes destroyed. His skill and courage contributed greatly to the success of this engagement and were in keeping with the highest traditions of the Naval Service.

M. A. MITSCHER
Vice Admiral, U. S. Navy

Temporary Citation

Angel In The Cockpit

THE SECRETARY OF THE NAVY
WASHINGTON

The President of the United States takes pleasure in presenting the GOLD STAR in lieu of the Fourth Air Medal to

**LIEUTENANT COMMANDER ARTHUR RAY HAWKINS
UNITED STATES NAVY**

for service as set forth in the following

CITATION:

"For meritorious achievement in aerial flight as Pilot of a Fighter Plane in Fighter Squadron ONE HUNDRED NINETY ONE, on board the U.S.S. PRINCETON, during operations against enemy aggressor forces in Korea from 6 December 1950 to 20 March 1951. Completing twenty missions during this period, Lieutenant Commander,(then Lieutenant) Hawkins participated in armed reconnaissance, photo-escort and target combat air patrols. Pressing home daring attacks in the face of hostile antiaircraft fire, he contributed materially to the success of his squadron in the infliction of extensive damage upon enemy lines of communication, transportation facilities, supply centers and troop concentrations, thereby upholding the highest traditions of the United States Naval Service."

For the President,

Secretary of the Navy

UNITED STATES PACIFIC FLEET
COMMANDER CARRIER DIVISION THREE

In the name of the President of the United States, the Commander Carrier Division THREE, United States Pacific Fleet, takes pleasure in presenting the GOLD STAR in lieu of a third AIR MEDAL to

LIEUTENANT (JUNIOR GRADE) ARTHUR RAY HAWKINS
UNITED STATES NAVAL RESERVE

for series of meritorious acts while participating in aerial flight

From 10 July 1945
To 9 August 1945.

Basis for award:

Fifth flight in a combat area where enemy anti-aircraft fire was expected to be effective or where enemy aircraft patrols usually occurred.

T. L. SPRAGUE,
Rear Admiral, U. S. Navy

Angel In The Cockpit

THE SECRETARY OF THE NAVY
WASHINGTON

    The President of the United States takes pleasure in presenting the GOLD STAR in lieu of the Third Air Medal to

LIEUTENANT ARTHUR RAY HAWKINS
UNITED STATES NAVY

for service as set forth in the following

CITATION:

    "For meritorious achievement in aerial flight as Pilot of a Fighter Plane in Fighting Squadron THIRTY ONE, attached to the U.S.S. BELLEAU WOOD, during operations against enemy forces in the vicinity of the Japanese Homeland from July 10 to August 9, 1945. Completing five combat missions during this period, Lieutenant (then Lieutenant, Junior Grade,) Hawkins contributed materially to the success of his squadron in the infliction of extensive damage on enemy grounded planes, shipping facilities and other strategic ground targets. His skill and courage in the face of hostile antiaircraft fire were in keeping with the highest traditions of the United States Naval Service."

For the President,

James Forrestal
Secretary of the Navy

THE SECRETARY OF THE NAVY
WASHINGTON

The President of the United States takes pleasure in presenting the GOLD STAR in lieu of Second Air Medal to

**LIEUTENANT ARTHUR RAY HAWKINS
UNITED STATES NAVAL RESERVE**

for service as set forth in the following

CITATION:

"For meritorious achievement in aerial flight as Pilot of a Fighting Plane in Fighting Squadron THIRTY-ONE, attached to the U.S.S. CABOT, in action against enemy Japanese forces in the vicinity of the Philippine Islands, September 12, 1944. Participating in an attack against enemy shipping, Lieutenant (then Lieutenant, Junior Grade,) Hawkins pressed home several low-altitude strafing runs through an intense enemy barrage to explode and sink a small ammunition-laden enemy freighter. His courage, initiative and devotion to duty were in keeping with the highest traditions of the United States Naval Service."

For the President,

James Forrestal
Secretary of the Navy

Chapter Eleven

Return to the Regular Navy

When I became a civilian again in 1945, I was one of thousands of veterans returning homes to the State of Texas. The government was doing everything possible to make our return to civilian life as smooth as possible. Jobs were at a premium and competition for them was great. Most veterans took this mad search for a job with a touch of good humor. You might hear one of them say, "If I can't find a job, I can always trade in my good conduct medal for a cup of coffee." The government had three programs that gave the returning Veterans a big boost in their return to civilian life.

One program allowed each veteran unemployment compensation for five to eight weeks to give him some assistance in getting himself organized and finding a job.

Another program was a Veteran's Guaranteed Home Loan. This allowed any veteran to borrow money to buy a house, with the government guaranteeing the loan. The third program was a Veterans Education Scholarship that paid for college or technical training.

It was the Education Scholarship Program that I applied for. I went about registering for college so I could finish work on my degree. As I made preparations for getting back into school, I received a letter from the Bureau of Naval Personnel. The letter said that I had been selected for a commission in the Regular Navy. The letter stated that if I were to accept, I should report to the Eighth Naval District Headquarters in New Orleans, Louisiana, for a flight physical. If I passed the physical, I would be sworn into the Regular Navy with the rank of Lieutenant.

Angel In The Cockpit

Back in 1942, I had enlisted in the Naval Reserve, rather than the "Regular" Navy. A lot of us did - it seemed to make very little difference with a war going on. Now I was being offered the same rank I held when I was discharged from the reserves and I could expect further active duty. I thought about it long and hard. After much soul searching and considering every plus and minus of such an important decision, I decided I would accept the offer and return to the Regular Navy. Little did I realize, as I raised my hand to accept this commission, that I was embarking on the continuation of a career that would span a period of thirty-one years.

I was ready to get back in the cockpit, ready to step aboard one of the big, new Essex class fleet carriers.

But that was not to be.

My orders said nothing about a carrier. Instead, I was to report to the Commanding Officer of the *USS Portsmouth*, a light cruiser, where I would assume the position of Senior Aviator of the aviation detachment on that vessel.

CL-102, the ***USS Portsmouth***, was the third ship in the American Navy to bear that name. She was a *Cleveland* class light cruiser, armed with a large number of small caliber guns to provide dense anti-aircraft fire but lightly armored. This class was specifically designed for the demands of carrier warfare. The *Portsmouth's* keel was laid down in June of 1943 and she was commissioned in June of 1945, just barely too late to get into the war. She spent the next few years deployed on "show the flag" missions, spent another year doing Naval Reserve training cruises and was decommissioned in 1949 after a career of only four years.

As William Bendix used to say in the old radio show, *The Life of Riley*, "What a revolting development this turned out to be."

What was I doing here? I was a fighter pilot – a member of the elite, the epitome of combat aviation. Surely a mistake had been made. How could the Navy expect me to fly a small seaplane from the fantail of a light cruiser? I mean, when you think about it, the Kingfisher float plane felt like a horse and buggy alongside the Hellcat.

I had a feeling that this change was not going to be easy, and I began wondering if, perhaps I hadn't made a mistake by accepting a regular commission.

The **OS2U, Kingfisher**, was the first metal single-wing seaplane and the last single engine float plane built for the US Navy. It replaced earlier wood and canvas biplane models beginning in 1940. Its maximum speed was less than half that of an F6F Hellcat and it was not very maneuverable due to the enormous float attached to the bottom. Still these planes did yeoman service during World War II.

Actually, though it wasn't something I wanted to think about, I was getting back to the original concept of naval aviation with this assignment. Battleship and cruiser launched scout planes were the earliest form of naval aviation. The original purpose was to provide scouting for the capital ships, so they could find the enemy battle line and pound it with their big guns. When the war started, it quickly became obvious that modern carriers made its original purpose redundant. The Kingfishers were switched to anti-submarine duties and to search and rescue. And in that capacity, the Kingfisher served very well. Hundreds of downed pilots owe their lives to the Kingfishers.

The first thing I had to do was master the launch. At first I didn't think it would be all that difficult. I was a qualified carrier pilot, after all.

"Hawk, you ever thought you'd like to work for the circus?" one of the other aviators asked.

"Work for the circus? What do you mean?"

"After you launch, you'll be qualified to work for the circus," he said. He laughed. "You can be one of those guys who gets fired out of a cannon."

The others laughed as well, but I had no idea what they were talking about.

I learned quickly.

No wide flight deck here, the cruiser had two catapults on its fantail, pointing aft. Each catapult was about thirty feet in length. A bag of black powder, the same as used to fire the cruiser's big guns, was placed into a chamber on the catapult. When the powder was fired the energy from the blast threw the plane down the catapult and abruptly into the air.

As my head was snapped back by the detonation of the powder charge, I realized what they were talking about. I really was being fired from a cannon.

After getting into the air and completing a mission, the matter of getting back aboard the ship wasn't an easy task either. With the ship operating at sea, where the seas are often very rough and choppy, close cooperation between the pilot and the ship is a must. I was briefed that, for my landing the ship will make a sharp turn across the wind line, creating a slick, or smooth space, on the water. I would then land into the wind, using the slick as the touchdown point.

I managed to do that so easily that a big smile broke out. "Piece of cake," I said aloud.

"Stand by for recovery," I heard in my headset.

"Recovery?"

Even as I was wondering what that meant, a boom was lowered to tow a rope sled in the water alongside and I taxied forward onto the sled. A hook on the bottom of the plane's float caught onto the rope sled, then a huge crane lowered a hook and I shut off the engine, stood up on the seat and attached the hook to the lifting sling on the aircraft. The plane was then hoisted back aboard and placed on the catapult.

It all went well enough the first time, but that wasn't always the case. In very rough seas, the plane would be tossed off the sled and would slowly drift away from the ship as it continued forward. Then I would have to make a mad scramble to get back into the cockpit, get the plane started and taxi back onto the sled.

Getting the engine re-started, when the plane was being tossed around in a rough sea, was not a simple job. The plane's starter has a breach into which you placed a black powder shell, somewhat like a shotgun shell, and fired it. This turned the plane's engine over and you hoped to catch a start. Each aircraft has a supply of only five of these shells. So after five attempts and no start, you are in dire need of outside assistance. Somehow, even in the roughest seas, I managed to get the engine started. This was always a relief as it saved me the embarrassment of the ship having to put a whaleboat in the water to tow the plane back onto the sled.

Angel In The Cockpit

<u>*Recovery Operation for the OS2U Kingfisher*</u>

Operating procedures from a cruiser were a far cry from what I had used when flying from a carrier. I accepted the challenge and as my tour progressed, I learned to enjoy every minute of flying from the *Portsmouth* over the next eighteen months.

During this period we made two six-month deployments to the Mediterranean Sea. This was the start of the Cold War and our sole mission was to "show the flag" in this part of the world. This we did very well. In the company of other US capital ships, we visited all of the major cities along the Mediterranean coast.

The ships would anchor in the harbor or tie up to a pier and each ship would be brilliantly lit with lights that came to be known as "Mediterranean Lights." The ships were lit to advertise our presence and power to the local inhabitants. The US Navy had done much the same thing on many other occasions. Commodore Perry took his ships into Tokyo Harbor in 1883 and

'84 to impress the Japanese to open up their country to foreign trade. President Theodore Roosevelt sent the "Great White Fleet" around the world in 1907-9 to announce our presence on the world

    Completing my eighteen-month tour in June of 1948, I received orders to report to the Instructors Advanced Training Unit (IATU) in Jacksonville, Florida. After reporting aboard NAS Jacksonville, I learned that the Navy's Flight Demonstration Team, the Blue Angels, was attached to IATU. It was my luck to be reporting at a time when one of the members of the Blue Angels was completing his tour and would be leaving the team. The Commander of the "Blues", Lieutenant Commander Johnny Magda, asked me if I would like to join the Team and he did not have to ask twice. To be a member of the Blue Angels with their type of precision flying, demonstrating maneuvers at low altitude in close formation was a dream come true for any Navy or Marine Corps pilot.

    I can't believe that anyone reading these words would not be acquainted with the Blue Angels, but, just in case there is, I'll explain what they are. The Blue Angels US Navy Flight Demonstration Team is made up of six pilots that fly aerial demonstrations at airports around the world.

    Admiral Chester W. Nimitz was the Commander-in-Chief of the Pacific Fleet during World War II and the architect of America's "island hopping" campaign across the Pacific. In 1946, Admiral Nimitz was Chief of Naval Operations, the highest rung on the Navy ladder. With the war over, the nation was contemplating its leadership role in a new world order. It was a time of great changes. Germany and Japan had been defeated, but new tensions were rising with our former allies in the USSR. The technology of defense was changing too with the advent of nuclear weapons.

Angel In The Cockpit

And yet, despite the crucial role played by naval aviation against the Japanese in the Pacific, there were some in government who wished to save money by limiting the Navy's air arm. Unfortunately, with the birth of the U.S. Air Force a coming event, their arguments sounded increasingly convincing to a public tired of war and tired of the expense of maintaining a large military.

It was the Admiral's intention to counter that, by keeping the public interested in naval aviation. To that end he issued a directive establishing a naval flight demonstration team. The demonstration team got their nickname on a trip to New York. Lieutenant Maurice Wickendoll saw a reference to the famous Blue Angel nightclub in a New Yorker magazine. He immediately christened the team the Blue Angles.

For those of you who have seen the Blue Angels perform, I do not have to tell you how beautiful and breathtaking the performance is. Maneuvers such as loops, rolls, Cuban eights, bomb bursts, etc., all done in diamond, echelon or delta formation, are performed at low altitude, directly in front of the spectators, with as little as twenty-four inches separating the planes in the formation. If you haven't seen the Blue Angels, I recommend you do so. There are some fifty-two shows each year in different cities around the world.

The year I joined the team, the "Blues," flying the F8F Bearcat flew over fifty air shows to an estimated four million spectators. One air show over Coney Island in New York City drew an audience of more than a million people.

The Grumman **F8F, Bearcat**, was the last piston-engine fighter purchased by the US Navy. Designed in 1943 and first flown in 1944, it entered service at the very end of World War 2. It was the last evolution of Grumman's "Cat" series. It used the same powerful engine as the Hellcat, but with a smaller and lighter frame. This resulted in greatly improved performance with higher level speed and a greatly improved rate of climb. Pilots referred to the Bearcat as a "hotrod" because of its snappy performance.

Not long after I joined the team, the Blue Angels were reassigned from NAS Jacksonville to NAS Corpus Christi in Texas. It was nice to be back in Texas once more and relatively near home.

In June of 1949, the days of the propeller driven Bearcat were becoming a thing of the past. The Blue Angels switched to the Navy's newest operational jet aircraft, the Grumman F9F-2 Panther. We went to the Grumman Plant in Beth Paige, New York and under the tutelage of the Grumman test pilots, the six of us were checked out in the Panther. After a short air show for the employees of Grumman, we returned to Corpus Christi.

> Grumman's **F9F, Panther**, was the first jet fighter to reach widespread service with the US Navy. It continued the Grumman tradition of producing rugged, dependable aircraft. While not the hottest fighter around, it proved its utility with ground support missions. Entering service in 1949, it served as the Navy's mainstay during the Korean War and survived into the late fifties.

Flying the Panther jets, we flew thirty-eight shows in different cities around the United States, up until June 1950. On June 25th, 1950, things changed once again. Behind a thunderous artillery barrage, the North Korean Army came pouring south of the 38th parallel. The Korean War had begun.

Congress and the Department of Defense had deeply cut the Navy budget following World War II. The Navy found itself with only a bare minimum of jet fighter squadrons and very few jet-trained pilots when the Korean War started. It was decided that the Blue Angels, with our trained jet pilots and enlisted crew, would form the nucleus for a jet fighter squadron for aircraft carrier duty in Korea. I had been in the Navy less than ten years, and was about to take part in my second war.

We flew our last air show at the U.S. Naval Air Station Dallas, Texas, on 29 and 30 July 1950. After the air show in Dallas, we flew to San Diego, California, where we reported to the Commander, Fleet Air Pacific (COMAIRPAC). We received written orders from COMAIRPAC to proceed and report to the Commanding Officer of Fighting Squadron 191 (VF-191), based at the Naval Air Station, Moffett Field, California. Our Skipper, Commander Johnny Magda, received orders that directed him to report and assume command of Fighting Squadron 191. The "Blue Angels" ground officers and enlisted crew received dispatch orders to report to the Commanding Officer of VF-191 on or before 15 August 1950.

Not letting any grass grow under our feet we flew into Moffett Field on 1 August 1950 and reported aboard. The six of us, using the six Blue Angels aircraft, started ground school and cockpit checkouts for all the other pilots of VF-191. The pilots had been flying the prop driven Bearcat and were eager to get into the air in the Panther jet. We received twelve new Panthers and our Blue Angels ground officers and enlisted crew reported aboard, so things were ready to change this squadron over from props to jets.

Each Blue Angels pilot was assigned to take a lead in getting the newly assigned pilots checked out in the Panther as quickly as possible. This phase of the training went smoothly. Due to the urgent need for more aircraft carriers on the Korean front, we completed what was supposed to be a six-month training syllabus, in gunnery, bombing, rockets, tactics, instruments, navigation, radio, night flying and carrier qualifications, in a short three-months.

Another indication of the reductions in the military budget following World War II was that a carrier for our air group 19 had to be brought out of "moth balls" where it had been stored in 1949. Our carrier the, *USS Princeton*, was being outfitted at the Naval Shipyard in Bremerton, Washington. It became the thankless task of Captain Bill Gallery to turn the *Princeton* into a fighting ship and that he did. Let me say here, that a better Skipper never took the helm of a fighting carrier. He had the internal operations of the ship in fighting trim and on October 9, 1950, took the air group on board to fine tune the operations of the ship and the air group working together as a single fighting unit.

> The **USS Princeton**, CV-37, was commissioned in November of 1945. It was a *Ticonderoga* class fleet carrier, similar in performance to the earlier Essex class but with slightly increased length and anti-aircraft armament. She served three tours in Korea and, after numerous changes of duty served on into 1970 as an amphibious assault ship.

For the rest of October, the air group continued its operations with the carrier, until 9 November, when we all said our goodbyes, went aboard the carrier and set sail for Hawaii. On our three-day run to Hawaii there were no flight operations, which gave us time to meet and get to know the members of our sister squadrons of the air group. Because of our intensive training, there had been no time to socialize and get to know the members of the other squadrons. air group 19 was made up of three fighter squadrons, VF-191 (F9F jets), VF-192 and 193 (F8F props), one bombing squadron, VA-195 (props), plus two to three-plane detachments from VC Squadrons 3, 11 and 35 flying specially

Angel In The Cockpit

equipped aircraft for night combat operations of all kinds and antisubmarine warfare. We also had several planes from VC-61 for photo recon. Our photo unit was the first jet photo unit to enter combat.

Upon arrival in Hawaiian waters, we did not go in to dock but stayed in the operating area for eight days where we continued our carrier qualifications and made numerous live ammunition strikes on Kahoolowe Island. This important eight days of training gave the air group a chance to smooth out tactics and brought the people together into a single fighting unit.

The ship went into Honolulu and docked at Pearl Harbor where we had a pleasant weekend liberty. Then it was back into the operating area where we continued our strikes on Kahoolowe and sharpened up our carrier landings and deck operations. The ship personnel used the time to practice their skills at weapon loading, fire fighting, damage control and flight deck operations.

All hands felt that we were well trained and all were ready to get on with it and apply this training in actual combat. The ship returned to Pearl Harbor where we spent Thanksgiving Day. Two days later we were on the high seas again, on our way to Sasebo, Japan. The war in Korea had been progressing very well so there was no cause for hurry. The ship was steaming along at a conservative fifteen knots, and we looked forward to several restful days as we made our way to Sasebo, Japan. On our first day at sea this all changed as the *Princeton* received dispatch orders to proceed at flank speed to the Korean War zone. We made a quick fueling stop in Sasebo, then it was up anchor and into the combat zone where the war was on in earnest for air group 19.

I feel that here I should cover what had been happening in the combat zone up to and until the time of our arrival in the combat area. After fighting began on June 25th, President Truman uttered his famous quote of, "We've got to stop the sons of bitches no matter what, and that's all there is to it." Truman committed the United States to intervene in the conflict.

He made this decision without seeking advice from the National Security Council or seeking approval from Congress. He made this decision, based on his constitutional authority as Commander-in-Chief of the military. He laid down the mission of our armed forces that could have been called a mission of "status quo." The mission stated that the North Korean forces were to be driven out of South Korea and our forces were not to cross above the 38th parallel, the border between North and South Korea. This was the same mandate given to the United Nations Forces as the UN entered the conflict. To accomplish this mission General Douglas MacArthur, of the Far Eastern Command, was put in charge of the United States and United Nations forces in Korea.

The 24th Infantry Division, with close air support sorties from the aircraft carrier *USS Valley Forge* and a British aircraft carrier, plus support from the Far Eastern Air Force flying out of Japan, were able to brunt the initial surge of the North Korean forces. Still the South Korean and US forces were driven back into a perimeter around the port of Pusan where they grimly held on waiting for reinforcements.

Additional forces were on the way and the war took a sudden turn with their arrival. As more men poured into the Pusan perimeter the UN forces began to stabilize the battle and push the North Koreans back. Then, on September 15, the U.S. Tenth Corps landed at Inchon, far in the rear of the North Korean Army. The successful amphibious landings at Inchon cut off the North Korean forces in South Korea. With the Eighth Army's break out from the Pusan Perimeter, a rapid drive north began.

Angel In The Cockpit

These successes gave cause for President Truman to modify the mission of our forces, directing that the North Korean Army would be pursued above the 38th Parallel and destroyed. However, he again put limitations on our forces, ordering that they were not to cross over the North Korean border into Manchuria or the Soviet Union under any circumstances. He also directed General MacArthur to use only South Korean troops in any engagements near the northern border. The United Nations passed a resolution approving this mission change.

The President was attempting to ensure that we did not get into a wider ground war in the Far East, especially not with China or the Soviet Union. General MacArthur told the President that he believed China would not enter the conflict if we continued our drive north to the border.

The Chinese had already infiltrated some 250,000 troops into North Korea. They had covertly taken up positions on the mountain ridges overlooking the valleys where our troops were advancing. Late on 25 November 1950, the Chinese troops began their attack south. They pushed through the South Korean Army's II Corps and devastated the right flank of the Eighth Army. It was at this turning point of the war that we on the *Princeton* received the dispatch to proceed to the war zone posthaste.

As I prepared to write about my experiences in Korea, the second of my wars, I wondered if I could recall it with the same intensity I recalled World War II. Once again, waiting until the Naval Air Museum in Pensacola was closed for the night, I wandered out on the floor among the many aircraft on display.

I wasn't wandering around aimlessly, I knew exactly where I was going, and I headed directly for the F-9F Panther.

If a machine that is designed to deliver death can be considered beautiful, it is my opinion that the F-9F Panther Jet is the most beautiful airplane ever made. As I had done earlier, with the Hellcat, I climbed into the cockpit of the Panther Jet, then sat there for a moment while memories flooded back.

I could smell the jet fuel, hear the sound of klaxons and loudspeakers, feel the roll and pitch of a carrier underway. Once again my memories had taken me to another time and place.

VF-191, Satan's Kittens, Unit Insignia

Chapter Twelve

Korea

The *Princeton* arrived on station and we started the first of many strikes that we flew during this so-called "Korean Police Action." As a part of Task Force 77, our first mission was to support the First Marine Division and elements of the Tenth Army Corps who were trapped at the Chosin reservoir, cut off by the Chinese advance. They were being hit by artillery fire at a murderous rate, raining down on them from the high ground held by the Chinese. For the next three weeks we flew continuous close-air support for the embattled marines and soldiers. Heavy snow and low clouds hampered our initial efforts but the weather cleared and we launched continuous strikes, day and night.

These attacks concentrated on the Chinese troops occupying the high ground. Tank after tank of the feared napalm was dropped to burn away the mountainsides and thwart their artillery's hammering of our troops. Our jets ranged far north on interdiction flights to suppress the support and supplies flowing out of Manchuria and the Soviet Union.

One flight that I made north, past the Chosin reservoir, sticks out in my memories. I had been sent out on an interdiction mission to attack the enemy's vehicles. I was armed with six 5" rockets and a full load of ammunition for my .20 millimeter cannons. I used two of my rockets to blow a locomotive off the tracks as it hauled supplies south. The remaining rockets had gone into a North Korean tank that I caught coming down a steep mountain road. The last I saw of the tank, it was tumbling over a ledge to the ground some three hundred feet below.

I was searching for additional targets when I spotted what looked like five to ten thousand Chinese troops crossing the ice of the frozen reservoir. On my first pass over the troops, they all squatted down and covered up with their white parkas to camouflage themselves in the snow that lay on the ice. I only had my 20-millimeter guns to attack with but I made three passes on the Chinese troops and expended all my remaining ammunition on them.

I could tell they were well-trained troops as not once, on any of my three attacks, did any of them break ranks and scatter. They just held their position and took everything I was dishing out. It was only an estimate, but in my report, I felt it safe to say that at least several hundred never made it across the reservoir after my attack. With all my ammunition expended, I reported the advancing troops to my home base. As I returned to the *Princeton*, I passed a strike heading for the reservoir to ensure the enemy troops did not get to finish their run across the ice without opposition.

Our support flights continued around the clock to give the Marines and Army troops close-air support as they fought their way, inch by inch, out of the trap. The press was making headlines about the Marines being in retreat from Chosin. The Marines retort to this was, "No way! We are just attacking in a different direction."

Slowly they fought their way south from the Chosin reservoir, through Hagaru-ri, Chanjin, Hamhung and finally to Hungnam where ships were waiting to take them aboard and out of harms way.

Angel In The Cockpit

This had been a bloody operation with casualties running into the thousands. By pure grit and determination, plus untold acts of heroism, the Marines and Army troops walked out of the Chosin trap over the dead bodies of some 40,000 Chinese soldiers. They made it to Hungnam on 24 December 1950. As the ships carrying our troops pulled away, some heavy equipment and rolling stock had to be left behind. When the ships reached a safe distance from the dock, explosives were detonated and the port of Hungnam disappeared from the face of the earth.

With the Marines safely off the beachhead our job had only begun. So on Christmas day, the *Princeton* and the other carriers in Task Force 77 launched an all-out effort to stem the flow of troops and equipment rolling south out of Communist China. These strikes pounded the cities of Koto-ri, Hagaru-ri, Sinpo and Wonson, day and night. For our air group, these strikes lasted through 6 January, 1951. By then the *Princeton*, fresh out of "moth balls", was in dire need of some repairs. We steamed to the shipyard in Sasebo, Japan for this work. The ten days that were required to complete the repairs gave a welcome rest to all hands. Our time in Sasebo passed rapidly and all too soon, we returned to the combat zone.

On our return to the line, Air Group 19 took up its old job of close-air support for the ground troops and interdiction strikes to stop the support flowing from the north. The second Communist offensive had begun and our planes, along with other groups present, launched an all out effort in support of the ground forces. We bombed, strafed and napalmed the enemy along the front lines, under the direction of the Marine, Army and Air Force Ground Controllers. One flight from the air group was credited with destroying an estimated 2,300 enemy troops with fragmentation bombs and napalm.

Along with our close-air support flights we were also bombing bridges on all highway and railroad routes leading from the north. By dropping the bridge spans we were slowing the movement of rolling stock and diverting manpower from the front lines to the repair of bridges.

To catch the trucks and trains that operated at night and hid in tunnels by day, we developed a "tunnel busting" technique. This technique entailed a low altitude run in toward the mouth of the tunnel and the release of a delayed fused bomb at a pre-selected speed and altitude. The bomb carried on into the mouth of the tunnel as the pilot made a sharp right or left clearing turn to get away. If the speed of the bomb is not enough to reach the tunnel it might detonate outside the tunnel and catch the aircraft as it tried to get away – dangerous work.

The Communist offensive was an all-out effort to overrun the city of Seoul so our ground support effort shifted to the western part of South Korea. The offensive was thwarted and our troops began to make bloody headway back toward the 38th parallel.

Since we had been on the front line for a month of night and day operations, the *Princeton* pulled out for replenishment and some minor repairs. This gave us a chance for a six-day shore leave in Yokosuka, Japan. Yokosuka was great, but six days was over in what seemed like a microsecond and we were back on station with Task Force 77 on 19 February.

With our troops on the ground holding their own, our area of operations was moved well north into North Korea. We were assigned interdiction of all routes leading south. If it moved we were to destroy it. We began hitting bridges, trucks, trains and anything that could possibly carry troops or supplies south. Our night hecklers started picking off trains as they rolled south. Our "tunnel busters" blasted the ones that escaped to hide in tunnels out the next morning.

I almost created an international incident on one of my interdiction flights. My wingman and I were interdicting the route that runs the entire length of the North Korean east coast. The weather was poor, and we were operating under a very low overcast. Targets were plentiful, as I'm sure they thought we wouldn't be out in this kind of weather. Because of the low clouds and our concentration on attacking the plentiful targets, we were unaware that we were about to reach the northern border. All of a sudden, under this 500-foot ceiling we found ourselves over a large metropolitan city. Realizing that there was no such city on our North Korean route, we did a violent turn and departed from Vladivostok, USSR in a hurry. Needless to say, this was not mentioned in our debriefing when we returned to base. Nor was there ever a complaint of Russia's airspace being violated.

The accelerated interdiction campaign was proving to be a success; we had slowed supplies and equipment to a trickle. It had come at a great price though, since we had lost three pilots during this phase. It was doubly hard on us of Fighting Squadron -191, as we lost our Skipper, Commander Johnny Magda, on a strike over Tanchon, North Korea. These three loses brought the air group's total pilots lost to fifteen since we entered combat on 5 December 1950. The air group was hit hard by these losses but we were determined to keep up our effort to give our troops on the front lines all the support they needed and to prevent supplies from moving south.

We of the jet squadron had lobbied the Admiral ever since we came aboard to allow the jets to carry bombs and assist in the bridge busting. With the loss of our Skipper we redoubled this lobbying effort. The Admiral was hesitant because this had never been done before in combat and the catapults on the

Princeton were hydraulic. These old style catapults did not deliver the launching power of the steam catapults planned for future carriers. However, the Admiral relented and gave the go ahead to give it a try.

Because I was the first to launch, I was the guinea pig, and on 2 April 1950, my plane was loaded with six 250-pound bombs and I taxied onto the starboard catapult. The Catapult Officer signaled, and I applied full power. With a salute from me the Catapult Officer reached forward, touched the deck and the catapult fired. I'm sure that the Admiral, the Skipper of the *Princeton* and all those watching the launch from "vulture's row" were holding their breaths, awaiting the results. The violent g-forces from the shot threw my body hard back against the seat as the plane hurtled down the catapult track and lifted effortlessly into the air. I climbed for altitude where I tested the flight characteristics of the aircraft with the bombs on board. I reported to base that the plane handled normally and asked that the second bomb loaded plane be launched.

We joined up and proceeded to our assigned target. With our delayed-action-fused bombs we attacked three bridges. We knocked out the underpinning of each and left the bridge spans on the ground. We returned to base with the knowledge that we had proven a new combat use for our jet aircraft. One that would help us immensely in our stepped up interdiction campaign against the Communists.

After six long weeks of round the clock interdiction strikes, we were a weary group when we left the combat area for another ten-day rest at Yokosuka, Japan. We were well into our leave time when word was received that we were needed back on the line. It was like pulling teeth, but back we went. By 19 April 1950, we were again in action doing more of the same.

The weather had turned sour but we plugged ahead in close-air support for the ground troops as they slugged their way toward the 38th parallel. Our jets were ranging far north on their interdiction routes. Six trains were reported heading south in a desperate effort to supply the Communist forces as they made ready for their third big offensive. We launched special strikes against the six trains and stopped five of then on their tracks. The sixth train made it to apparent safety in a tunnel. Our "tunnel-busters" changed all that when we plugged the tunnel at both ends. This stopped any train traffic from ever running again on this section of the Kowan railroad line.

Our direct support of the ground operations continued at a fast pace. The jet squadron struck the northern part of North Korea, knocking off trains, trucks and any and all rolling stock carrying troops or supplies. In this phase of our operation the antiaircraft fire was heavy, and it was to our sorrow that we lost two pilots to this murderous fire. These losses were extremely hard to take but we had to live with it. We knew that our troops on the ground could use all the support we could give them and that we were making the enemy pay dearly.

It was of just such a mission that James A. Michener wrote his novel, *Bridges of Toko Ri*. In it, he has one of his characters ask, "Where do we get such men?"

As I watched the men of my squadron face the heavy anti-aircraft fire again and again, I often wondered the same thing. Where did we get such men?

Our air group was on our last leg of our combat tour. A rotation policy had been established. After six months in combat, an air group would be relieved and returned to the States. We were looking forward to being relieved sometime in the middle of May with great expectations.

Before leaving the area our Skyraider squadron made its now famous torpedo attack on the Hwachon Dam on 7 May. The dam was strategically important since the enemy could thwart our troop movements by flooding the Pukhan River or aid their own forces by reducing the depth of the river. The dam was ordered destroyed and the job fell to our Skyraider squadron.

Design of the Douglas **AD-4, Skyraider**, was begun in 1944 to answer the Navy's requirement for a long-range, single-seat, multi-mission attack plane. Entering service in December of 1946, the AD-4 fulfilled these requirements admirably. It was able to carry tons of bombs, dozens of rockets or even torpedoes. The Skyraider was considered by many to be the finest ground support aircraft in the world during the Korean War. Its career carried on for more than two decades and the last Skyraider did not leave active service with the US Navy until 1971.

When it was decided that conventional bombs could not destroy the dam, torpedoes were selected for the job. This would be a first; air launched torpedoes had never been used in an attack against anything other than ships. Eight Skyraiders were loaded with torpedoes and launched for an attack on the dam. Flying low over the water the eight torpedoes were launched and six of them scored telling hits. The dam was breached, and gushing water flowed down the face of the dam, making it impossible to control the flow of the Pukhan River. This "first" was one of many for our air group and the *Princeton* during this combat tour.

On 17 May 1951 the *Princeton* pulled out of the line and headed for Yokosuka, Japan where the air group would be relieved. Late on that same day, the Chinese Communists' long-awaited third offensive began. The *Princeton* was almost in spitting distance of Yokosuka when we did a hundred and eighty-degree turn and reluctantly returned to the combat zone.

Even before we returned to our assigned position in Task Force 77, we started launching close air support strikes. The Eighth Army was receiving the brunt of the Communist push and they needed our help. This maximum effort on close air support lasted for a two long days. Our troops on the ground gained the upper hand and stopped the Communist offensive in its tracks. With the situation stabilized and with a message of gratitude from the Eighth Army Commander for our support, the *Princeton* again headed for Yokosuka.

We were all happy to be on our way to being relieved once again and we left the combat zone with a feeling of accomplishment. However, these last two days had not been without tragedy and deep sadness. We lost our air group Commander, Richard Merrick, to antiaircraft fire on a close air support mission east of Seoul, South Korea.

Also lost to antiaircraft fire was Lieutenant H.M. Hawkins who was flying a similar mission in the eastern section of Korea. Horace was not a relative of mine but having the same rank and last name, his loss created quite a bit of uneasiness back at my home when they learned a Lieutenant Hawkins was missing off the *Princeton*. These losses were extremely hard to take for all of us. We all had experienced that feeling of relief for having "made it" through six months of combat and we were on our way to be relieved. After being called back into combat, it was doubly sad that our comrades had died on their last combat mission on the day they were scheduled to return home.

This time the *Princeton* made it to Yokosuka and on 22 May 1951, air group 19 was relieved as air group 19X came aboard and took over our aircraft and spaces. We looked back on a six-month combat tour with pride in our accomplishments. We flew a total of 5,960 combat sorties, dropped 26,660 bombs, 2,998 tanks of napalm and fired millions of rounds of 20 millimeter and 50 caliber ammunition, plus thousands of five inch and HVAR rockets. All of this was done in support of our troops who were fighting a deadly, cold and bloody ground war.

They held the first thrust of the North Koreans as they attacked South Korea. They launched a counter offensive that had taken them to the northern borders of North Korea. They stood the brunt of the overt entry of a quarter million Chinese Communist troops into the battle. They withstood three major bloody offensives by the Chinese and were in a position to pushing the Communists back out of South Korea. We felt pride for being a part of all this.

air group 19 was officially relieved and sent gypsy-style back to the States, by ship and by plane, arriving without fanfare or recognition. Upon arrival in the States, air group 19 was assigned hangar space at Alameda, California, where the air group once again began the same old routine operation of reforming into a fighting unit. Alas, this reforming was not going to include me. I received orders to return to Naval Air Station, Corpus Christi, Texas. The Navy Department, realizing the need for a proven recruiting tool, had decided to reform the "Blue Angels". Two members of the past team, Pat Murphy and myself, were ordered to be a part of that reformation.

I was elated to be returning to the Blue Angels and their exciting style of flying, but I also felt much sadness at leaving the air group. I knew that the Group would reform in a hurry and be back on the front line. Deep inside, I wanted to be a part of it.

The air group did return and the bloody conflict in Korea continued for almost another year before a cease-fire was called, as negotiations for a truce got under way. These negotiations were a real "comedy act" with their first important decision being what kind of tables to use for the negotiations, square or round. These talks lasted until July 1953, when Truman's micromanaged, limited war came to an end. Status quo was regained and we left 30,000 troops behind to ensure the border was observed. To this day the troops remain.

This war has gone by many names – "Korean War", the "Korean Conflict", the "Korean Police Action" and the "United Nations War." Even today many call it the "Forgotten War," but believe me, the families of the 55,000 troops who died and those who fought in the action will never forget it.

Photo Album

Underway Replinishment for the Princeton

Angel In The Cockpit

Division Seven

VF-191 over San Francisco Bay

Angel In The Cockpit

<u>The Princeton in June of 1951</u>

<u>My division aboard the Princeton. I'm on the left</u>

Hungnam Goes Up!

Hwachon Reservoir before the attack - note the dam in the lower left corner.

Angel In The Cockpit

Hwachon Reservoir During the Attack

Hwachon Dam after the attack,
the dam site is in the left center of the photo.

Chapter Thirteen

Supersonic Ejection

With the Korean War behind me, I was detached from Fighting Squadron 191 along with Pat Murphy. We were directed to take part in the reforming of the Blue Angels Flight Demonstration Team. In November of 1951, after an enjoyable thirty day leave with my family, I reported into the Naval Air Advanced Training Command at the Naval Air Station, Corpus Christi, Texas.

Pat Murphy had already reported and Commander Roy "Butch" Voris was also there. Butch was the first leader of the Blue Angels when they were formed in 1946. He had been ordered to Corpus Christi to take the lead in the reformation effort.

The first order of business for the three of us was to select three more pilots to fill out the six-pilot roster. Along with the selection of the pilots, there was the crucial task of picking the twenty-two enlisted men that would form the maintenance crew.

Membership in the Blue Angels has always been on a voluntary basis. Back in the early days, the pilots on the team carried the most weight in the selection of pilots to fill the vacant slots. With the veterans making the selections, pilots of known flying skills and character could be chosen. Over the years this selection procedure has been refined, mandating type and total of flight hours and requiring fleet experience.

Whatever else the selection requires, the highly visible and unchallenged elements of professionalism, trust and honor must be considered when selecting every Blue Angels pilot. Pat and I chose two pilots who had reported into the Advanced Training Command from our old squadron, Fighting 191. We had flown our Korean War tour with Lieutenants Junior Grade Bud Wood and Buddy Rich. We knew they possessed the required skills and the character traits we needed.

Commander Voris chose Lieutenant Tom Jones, who he had served with before. Tom was serving in one of the Advanced Training Command Squadrons, which made it convenient for him. Bud Wood and Buddy Rich were ordered to report to the "Blues" immediately. Our selected Senior Chief, Barney Baxter, was on board handling the task of screening the volunteers for the maintenance crew.

While our selected officers and enlisted crew were receiving official orders and reporting aboard, test pilots from the Grumman plant in Beth Paige, New York, flew our six new F9F-5 Panther aircraft into Corpus Christi. The planes bore the familiar blue and gold paint job that had become so well known on past Blue Angel aircraft.

We had been assigned hangar and office space on the air station, and it was on the first day of December, 1951, that we began our flight and ground training to bring the Blue Angels back into being.

Having been in the fleet flying from aircraft carriers for the past year, all the pilots' instrument cards had expired. We knew that we would be flying through all kinds of weather to get to our scheduled demonstrations around the country and we could not get clearance to do it if we did not have our instrument tickets.

So along with our daily flying to perfect our routines, we all went through a four-week instrument flight course.

With the instrument course successfully completed, we set our priority on developing the maneuvers that would make up the demonstration routine. Our training had gone exceptionally well when disaster struck. The Midshipmen from the Naval Academy were in Corpus Christi on their field trip around the shore stations and fleet units of the Navy. We were asked to do a small demonstration for them while they were in Corpus Christi. The new make-up of the Blue Angels diamond formation was with Commander Voris as the leader, Pat Murphy on the right wing, I was on the left wing and Bud Wood was in the slot. We had been training in this formation, and all had been going well. We had done one practice demonstration over the Naval Air Station, Kingsville, Texas, and it had turned out exceptionally well, so we agreed to do the routine for the Midshipmen.

The demonstration was going very well. We had done a diamond roll, a loop and a full Cuban eight. As we cleared right, to position for the next maneuver, we came in from over the water and ended up over the white concrete ramp that surrounded the seaplane hangars lining the beachfront. The violent updraft generated by the heat from the white ramp caused the diamond formation to break up.

The two wingmen and the slot man came up through the formation ripping pieces off of Voris' airplane as we came through. Pat Murphy nicked and broke the running light off of Voris' right wing. As I came through I mangled Voris' left tip tank and ripped my right tip tank completely off. As Bud Wood came through the formation from the slot, he lost the nose section of his aircraft and badly damaged Voris' elevator and tail section.

With the nose section gone, Bud was able to get his aircraft to about twelve hundred feet. He was not able to control the aircraft, so he chose to eject. He ejected safely but at such a low altitude, he had no time to deploy his parachute. Bud hit the water and was killed.

The three of us still in the air were able to keep our mangled birds flying. Choosing to land at an airfield that had a longer runway than Corpus Christi, we flew to the Naval Air Station at Kingsville, Texas - only a short distance from Corpus Christi. The three of us managed to land our damaged airplanes safely and made our way back to Corpus Christi.

We were devastated by Bud's loss and the reformation of the Blue Angels took a terrible blow. With sorrow in our hearts, we knew that life must go on, so we returned to the task of reforming the Blue Angels. Lieutenant Junior Grade "Auz" Aslund was selected to fill Bud's billet and Buddy Rich moved into the slot position of the diamond formation.

With the arrival of a new aircraft and the repair of the damage on the other aircraft, training took on a feverish pace. Commander "Whitey" Feightner and Lieutenant Mac MacKnight joined the Blue Angels bringing along two F7U Cutlass aircraft. They joined us in our training, preparing to add the Cutlass into the solo routine of the demonstration.

> The Vought **F7U, Cutlass**, was an advanced aircraft for its day. Fast and nimble, it had the potential to be an excellent fighter. Unfortunately, maintenance problems spelled its doom. Troublesome repairs plagued it throughout its service life. Combined with high fuel consumption at top speed yielding limited range and an unfortunate tendency for the nose gear to collapse on landing these troubles saw it soon withdrawn from service. It did provide a painful learning experience.

Angel In The Cockpit

In June 1952 Commander Voris led us on our first air show at the Mid-South Navy Festival in Memphis, Tennessee. From this first air show through mid-December, he led us on some twenty-four more successful air shows around the United States. In mid-December, 1952, in a change of command ceremony, I assumed command of the Blue Angels.

Because of excessive maintenance problems the Cutlass solo had been dropped from the routine and "Whitey" Feightner had been ordered to other duty. MacKnight remained with the team and Lieutenant Junior Grade Frank Jones had replaced Lieutenant Tom Jones. The new make-up of the diamond formation was: me as leader, Murphy on right wing, Aslund on left wing, Rich in the slot, with Mac Knight and Jones as solo. Mac Knight would receive orders and be replaced by Lieutenant Junior Grade Daryl Crow about half-way through the season.

As the new team, we trained during the remaining days in December, up through 24 January 1953, when we flew our first show at Naval Air Station, New Orleans, Louisiana.

The success of this air show was the start of many that would follow. Up until 4 August 1953, we would visit twenty-four different show sites and fly thirty-nine separate demonstrations to viewing crowds of over a million and a half spectators. At one two day air show at Moffett Field, California, they drew crowds of 280,000 the first day and 250,000 the next day. Bay Shore highway that runs along side Moffett Field was filled with automobiles from half way to San Francisco down to San Jose. Cars were just parked and people were out watching the air show. There must have been another 20,000 spectators that were never counted among our audience.

I have only talked of the demonstrations held through the 4th of August 1953. My reason for this is that something happened on that day that would stay with me all my life and needs to be covered in more detail, as I relate my experiences with the Blue Angels. The happening on that day was a high altitude bail out that I made under some very harrowing circumstances. Back then, I wrote an article for the *Saturday Evening Post* that covers the bail out in vivid detail. I would like to repeat the article here.

BAILING OUT AT SUPER SONIC SPEED

Taking a quote from General Douglas MacArthur's famous speech, I would say, "Old Fighter Pilots never die, they just fade away." During my "fading away" period I logged over 5,000 hours, including combat in World War II and Korea. One thing about combat you go looking for trouble, so you're not surprised to find it. It's the unexpected that really curls your hair. I've never been more scared or nearer to death than I was on a flight way back on 4 August 1953. I had this jet fighter at 40,000 feet, cruising level. It was so safe, so easy; and then, over Mississippi, the plane went crazily supersonic and tried to kill me.

Back then I was the Leader of the Blue Angels and I had the Team on a cross-country flight. All six members were flying a comfortable line abreast, when my plane went out of control. It dived into an enormous outside loop - I was vertical - then I was upside down, hanging by my safety belt, and beginning to red out as centrifugal force whirled blood into my brain at tremendous pressure.

That would put the fear of God into any man, especially when you know that you're traveling faster than the speed of sound. If I was going to bail out, I'd have to go now, before I lost consciousness - now or never. But the slipstream outside my canopy was supersonic; plunging into those granite-hard shock waves might conceivably smash the life out of me. As of this time, in all the history of aviation, no one had pierced the sonic wall with only his body - bareheaded, so to speak. At least no one had survived to tell about it.

I remember thinking of all that; at the same time, I felt sorry that my plane was going to auger in and be destroyed. It was the F9F-6 Cougar. In 1953 it was the last word in Grumman-built Navy fighters - wings swept back, lots of fizz out the rear end, and a red-line speed above Mach 1.0. The F9F-6 Cougar was a new type, superseding the F9F-5 Panther. As soon as dash-six production started, the Blue Angels wanted to trade in their dash fives - all of a sudden the Panther was last year's airplane. Finally, after months of itching, we had the word that six Cougars were waiting for our team at the Grumman factory in Beth Paige, Long Island. We left our old jets at Corpus Christi, Texas and flew north in a Navy transport, arriving late in the day. The next morning we swarmed out to the factory, six eager guys. Texas here we come!

> The Grumman F9F-6, Cougar, was a step forward in Navy aircraft. When the high performance MIG-15 appeared over Korea, the Navy saw immediately that an improved fighter was required. Grumman responded with the F9F-6. With swept wings and a more powerful engine it fulfilled the requirements handily. It was a very "hot" bird with greatly improved speed and climb compared to its Panther predecessors. Entering service in November of 1952, the Blue Angels received some of the earliest planes.

But first we had to study the F9F-6 cockpit, noting how it differed from the F9F-5 layout. There were important changes in the elevator system. In the older Grumman, you had to take your hand off the throttle to adjust elevator trim tabs. In this one, there was a button on the control stick; you could trim nose up or nose down by flicking it with your thumb. Electric motors did the rest. There was an emergency trim-tab system, too, also electric.

Then, the Cougar had been given what was called a "flying tail." The idea behind it was fairly simple. You take a conventional tail, with its horizontal surfaces - a moveable elevator hinged to a rigid stabilizer. Now, unfreeze the stabilizer, design it to tilt up and down like the elevator, and provide a power drive. There's your flying tail. In effect, it gave a pilot a double-size elevator whenever he cut it in.

So we had skull practice. After that we took the Cougars up for routine flight-testing. The flying tail, we learned, was hardly needed at low altitudes, where the air was thick enough to give standard elevators a good bite. But at high altitude, in thin air, it was invaluable. We finished the hop well satisfied, bought the airplanes from Grumman and took off for home.

On the way, we stopped at Sewart Air Force Base in Smyrna, Tennessee, for fuel and lunch. So far, so good. Leaving Smyrna, it took us about twenty minutes to get climbed out and formed in line abreast. We weren't pushing our engines, but another hour would see us in Corpus Christi. Or so I thought. I had no premonition of danger. The controls felt a little sloppy, but that's normal at 40,000 feet. A normal stick movement isn't enough in skinny air. When you move the stick big, it's too much, you get into a lope, but nothing to worry about. I turned my head left, and right, to see the other planes. When I looked forward again, my nose had dropped a little below the horizon, that's no worry either, you ease back on the stick slightly, the nose rises, and there you are. But this time there was no response to stick movement. The nose stayed down. It went farther down, I thought I could recover by adjusting the elevator trim tab. It was already set a little nose-up, just enough for level cruise at altitude. I thumbed the button on my stick, feeding more nose-up trim. Not too much. The dive was getting steeper. My air speed was getting very high. I fed in more trim tab. No response. More trim tab, and more, until I had all of it. Still no response; the airplane was getting away from me, diving steeper and steeper; building up speed every moment. I heard one of the "Blues" call on the radio - it was Lieutenant Bud Rich's voice - "There goes Hawk; he's in trouble!"

Centrifugal force was pulling me out of my seat, and I realized that I was in the first arc of an outside loop. What had gone wrong? I had only seconds left to figure this out. Not the trim tab. Might be the flying tail, switched on accidentally. No, the switch was still at OFF position. The engine, then a sudden flame-out but the gauge shows I'm pulling 90 percent power - of course it might be stuck there - To test instrument response, I shoved the throttle forward. The gauge went to 95 percent; so power wasn't my trouble.

The dive angle was now about thirty-five degrees, and my speed was approaching a dangerous level. Mach meter and airspeed needles were wheeling around together. Another glance at the instrument panel showed that I was already past the speed of sound - and the needles were still winding up. Dive angle fifty degrees - vertical!

The loop's centrifugal force had me pinned up against the canopy, and a crimson haze began to cloud my vision. It was the first stage of a red-out. There was one last hope - - keep pressure on the stick, full nose-up trim, and switch on the flying tail.

I flipped the switch. And with that, the airplane tucked under, and I was upside down, hanging in my harness. Vision was going; consciousness would go next. There was just time enough left to jettison the plastic canopy and fire the explosive charge that would cannon me into space, seat and all.

I knew the bailout drill by heart. Depress the pre-ejection lever; it blows off the canopy and arms the explosive shell behind your seat. Draw your feet back into the stirrups. Reach overhead, grasp two handles and

Angel In The Cockpit

pull the protective curtain over your face. The last inch of pull will trigger a firing pin. Boom! Out you go.

But I couldn't get the sequence started. Hung up in the canopy as I was, my reach wasn't long enough to shove down the pre-ejection lever. Stretching to the utmost, I could just graze it with a fingertip. One last chance. Alongside my head was an emergency handle to be used only in desperate cases. It would arm the ejection seat. But it wouldn't blow off the canopy. To get out of this supersonic mantrap, I'd have to fire myself through thick plastic glass. I pulled the handle. How tough is my helmet? Duck down. Maybe the seat rails will punch a hole. I pulled down the face curtain.

When the ejection charge fired, I was four or five inches off the seat. It came up and hit me like a pile driver. Too stunned to feel anything, I went through the canopy, a limp bundle traveling faster than sound. When the momentary blackout passed, I found myself clawing for my ripcord in a groggy attempt to open my parachute. Then I thought, "How stupid! Wait until you slow down. A chute opened at this speed would be torn to shreds."

The seat and I were tumbling over and over, but that soon stopped, and I was sitting upright in space, falling with a lot of forward motion, like an artillery shell. It was then that I realized that I was bareheaded. The wind had torn away my face curtain, helmet and oxygen mask. No oxygen, my altitude was still above 30,000 feet - I'd gasp my life out if I opened the parachute and dangled up here. I decided to fall free for two or three miles, to get into breathable air as soon as possible. So I fell, keeping one hand on the trip that would jettison my seat, and the other on the ripcord handle.

Two or three miles? Why, in about four seconds the lack of oxygen was graying me out. If I blacked out entirely, I knew that I might never wake up in time to pop the chute. At an altitude later estimated as 29,000 feet, I opened my safety belt and pulled the ripcord. When the chute blossomed, it jerked the living fool out of me. The shock was so great that I thought the canopy had torn, but, looking up, I saw it was intact.

Next, I thought of my feet and legs. As far as I knew, I was the first Navy pilot to be fired through a canopy. But a lot of dummies had been shot through, in experiments, and I'd read the reports; most of them had feet torn off, legs shattered, heads bashed in. My head felt all right, and I saw that my feet were still attached to my legs.

The ground below was so far away that it didn't seem to be coming up at all. It was very quiet. The only sound was a soft whistling of air in my parachute and then I couldn't see the ground, or the parachute, or anything. My vision faded away. I seemed to be suspended in a gray fog. I needed oxygen.

After a while, I heard a jet go by. I was too grayed out to see it, but I knew it was one of the "Troops," following me down. I could think after a fashion, and hear, and feel - I remember feeling the intense cold. But I couldn't see. Then, finally, came the blackout. I came back to gray; sank into blackness once more; again regained gray consciousness. The blackouts scared me. If I could only hang on until I got down where there was oxygen pressure.

The chute drifted down through a layer of rough air that swung me from side to side. I was violently sick at my stomach. Mississippi got sprayed and I felt better.

Angel In The Cockpit

My vision cleared, and in a space of mental clarity I remembered a lesson from Navy flight training, about "grunt breathing." If you loose your oxygen mask in a high-altitude bailout," we were told, "take deep breaths, close your mouth and grunt hard. That will put pressure on the air in your lungs, and force oxygen into your blood stream."

I tried it, inhaling, holding it and straining to put on pressure. Pressure is the thing; there's oxygen at high altitude, but it's at low pressure. A few seconds after each grunt, my vision would improve for a while. Now I could see the jet. He was flying figure eight to stay with me, but keeping a safe distance so his jet blast wouldn't collapse my chute. I recognized the plane as an F9F-6. Where the four others were, I couldn't guess.

It was explained later: To begin, three jets were on my right, and two on my left, when my plane nosed over. Lieutenant Bud Rich, the first to see me go, dived on my tail and had my plane in sight all the way to the ground. He didn't see me bail out. Nobody did - I was a mere speck in an enormous sky.

Lieutenant Pat Murphy and Lieutenant (jg) Frank Jones went screaming down right behind Rich. That left Lieutenant Roland Aslund and Lieutenant (jg) Daryl Crow to circle around, putting out "Mayday" distress calls, holding 40,000 feet to get maximum range on their transmitters. They hoped ground stations could take radio bearings on them, and thus pinpoint the crash location. It worked too.

The Troops told me later that my plane completed only the first half of its outside loop. After it got on its back, it went down at a steep angle, augured in and exploded. Rich followed down - when he leveled out he was barely 500 feet off the ground - and saw the plane strike in a wooded area, doing no harm.

Murphy and Jones leveled off at 1,000 feet, radioed news of the crash to the troops topside, and started climbing back. Topside flashed the word to Barksdale Air Force Base in Shreveport, and Corpus Christi had it on a hot line before Murphy and Jones got high enough to see something glinting in the sun - me and my parachute.

For a minute, they mistook me for a high-altitude weather balloon. They still didn't know that I had bailed out. We met at 22,000 feet. Murphy stayed up there, feeding radio reports to the nearest military air base, while Jones flew a descending figure eight pattern along side me. It was a long, slow drop, and everybody was getting low on fuel. Aslund and Crow went into Barksdale and reported to NAS Corpus Christi by phone. Murphy and Rich landed at NAS Memphis and eventually, Frank Jones went there too.

The entire accident, including the slow float down, took about half an hour. It seemed even longer, hanging in the chute. I wanted to give Frank a wave, to let him know I was alive, but being starved for oxygen, I lacked the strength to lift an arm. I thought, "Well, I'll save energy and let him know later."

Grunt breathing kept me alive all the way down to 10,000 feet, and there I could breathe normally. At 5,000 feet, I was able to raise my arms in a semaphore "R" for "Roger" - O.K. The ground was coming up fast - woods, cotton patches, highways. I was drifting toward a country road, and I could see a pickup truck moving to intercept me.

I missed a barbed wire fence and landed in a cotton patch. The chute quietly collapsed on the ground. People from the truck came running. I felt too weak to get up right away. I told them to let me sit awhile. Jones buzzed us in the Cougar. Since I didn't feel like getting up just yet, I asked one of the men to signal for me. "Wave to him on the next pass so he'll know I'm all right."

Back came the jet, shrieking, and the man waved his hat. That didn't satisfy Frank, he could see me setting up, but I didn't look very lively. He came by again at 100 feet. I got on my feet, semaphoring "Roger" and a wave-off. He waggled his wings, and with drying tanks, went off on a beeline for NAS Memphis.

The people in the pickup drove me to the scene of the crash, about three miles away. I wanted to make sure the plane hadn't hurt anyone or destroyed property; and after that, I wanted the wreckage inspected for clues to the cause of my trouble. A rising column of smoke led us to a wooded area, where a crowd of people was standing around a deep crater. Fire smoldered in the pit my plane had dug, and chunks of metal were scattered everywhere. I asked if anyone had seen the tail or parts of it.

A man said, "I think its back over there," and he showed me a good piece of the tail. I asked him to see that no one picked up anything for a souvenir, and to phone the Marshal for a guard. He said he would attend to it. I was then driven to the small town of Pickens, Mississippi where I made my official call to the Duty Officer at Corpus.

It was arranged that a Mississippi highway patrol car would take me to a nearby airfield, where the "Blue Angels" transport would be waiting to fly me to NAS

Memphis. There was just time to see a local doctor. He taped up my ribs and gave me a tetanus booster shot for scratches he found on my legs. My neck felt sore, my thighs ached from the two-and-a-half-ton spanking the ejection seat had given me, and altogether I felt as if I'd played an hour of football against a rough team.

It was after dark when we landed at the Naval Air Station in Memphis. Rich, Murphy and Jones were waiting for me, and there was an ambulance I didn't need. But I had to go to the Navy hospital where they looked me over. I had nothing worse than this one bruised rib, so they told me to return in the morning for x-rays.

For a man who had been through a supersonic bailout, an unheard-of thing, I was in good shape. For instance, I might have frozen to death, floating so long in subzero temperatures at high altitude. Luckily, the slipstream hadn't torn off my shoes or gloves, and I was wearing my uniform under the flight suit. Only my ears were slightly frostbitten.

After x-rays the next day, I was flown back to Corpus Christi. The doctors at Corpus re-examined me. This time there was much emphasis on eyes and lungs, and I remember a psychologist dropping in, sitting around and popping little questions at me to get my mental attitude. They couldn't find any reason to ground me.

Yet it was six days before I flew the next air show. I was swamped with paper work. I had to write a formal accident report at once. Also, I owed the Bureau of Medicine and Surgery, in Washington, a report on my physical condition. Then, the safety experts wanted a special report written at great length.

I also had a phone call from the Naval Air Material Center (NAMC) in Philadelphia. In tests of escape procedures, they'd been firing dummies through plastic-glass canopies, and most of them could not take it. They asked, "Would I come east and talk over any ideas I might have"? I did visit NAMC, and on seeing the dummies, suggested that they be made more flexible, so they would squash down a little, as I had when the ejection seat walloped me, and go out with legs streamlining naturally after the torso. Perhaps I had the answer. But the big question was: why had my F9F-6 gone out of control in the first place? Was this an isolated case? Or was there a basic defect in the Cougar design, some hidden fault that would cause many more accidents?

We had the verdict very quickly. Cougars in general were safe, but I'd been unlucky enough to get one with a malfunction in the flying tail. Power for the up and down tilting is supplied by hydraulic pressure. In my plane, a very slow leak in a valve permitted a gradual build-up of pressure on the nose-down side of the system. The facts being known, a Navy order grounding all F9F-6's was lifted, on condition that they be flown with the stabilizer rigid, until Grumman could make a permanent fix.

I ordered another F9F-6 before the fix was made, and the Blue Angels continued practice using the five others. We were doubtful of the swept wing, at first, because sweeping is apt to hurt the precise control you get with a straight wing. And you'd better be precise, doing barrel rolls in tight formation at low altitude. However, the wing gave us no trouble at all. It was a fine airplane; in a way, you might say it saved my life. That emergency handle - the one that let me escape - existed at the time on only a few other aircraft. It was there because some of us wrote back from Korea and asked for it, suspecting that at least one of our buddies died because he couldn't eject himself by the normal procedure. Grumman pioneered the device in the F9F-6 and my experience prompted the Bureau of Aeronautics to order it put in all previous F9F's in the field.

That's the story as it appeared then and if I tried I could not tell it any better if I rewrote it today. I would like to say that after this story appeared in the *Saturday Evening Post*, the Editor received many letters. One in particular was by a lady from Houston, Texas, who wrote, "This young man must have had an Angel in the cockpit. The Good Lord is saving him for something, he better start looking for what it is."

Along this same thought pattern of divine intervention, it was some forty-nine years after the bail out that an aviation author friend of mine, Mr. Frank Gudaitis, did an excellent account of the Mach 1 bailout for the February, 2002 issue of the *Flight Journal* magazine. After the article ran, the Editor of *Flight Journal* received a letter from a Mr. Alec D. Van Ryan of Madison, Mississippi. The letter read:

"I have a touching and funny anecdote concerning Frank Gudaitis' excellent story on Ray Hawkins: "Punching out beyond Mach," in the February, 2002 issue. After reading the enthralling article about the first man to successfully eject from a U.S. jet fighter traveling at above the speed of sound, I wanted to share a story about this event from the perspective of those on the ground; it underlines the innocence of an early time.

"I work with a lady whose family lives in Pickens, Mississippi, the small town over which LCDR Hawkins' story

played out nearly 50 years ago. Her grandfather had apparently been working in a nearby cotton field when Hawkins was forced to eject. Her grandfather was not aware of the jet or the ejection, until several excited farm hands ran in from a nearby field. What they said and described was both amusing and touching. The workers shouted "that they must have been extremely good today because they just saw an angel with white wings float down from heaven."

"The event may have been a near technical disaster, but it was a spiritual affirmation for a lot of good people on the ground."

Well, be that as it may, divine intervention or not, as stated it was six days before our next air show. The air shows continued as we visited 17 separate show sites around the country, flying 27 flight demonstrations. It was on 21 February, 1954, at New Orleans Naval Air Station, the same place that I flew my first flight as Commander of the "Blue Angels," that I would fly my last flight as a "Blue." In an aerial change of command, in view of the air show spectators, I passed the lead to Commander "Zeke" Cormier and exited the demonstration. With orders in hand I was looking forward to my next assignment as a test pilot with Weapons Test Squadron Five.

Photo Album

*Official Photograph - US Navy Blue Angels
LCDR Ray Hawkins on right*

The Blue Angels: Rich, MacKnight, Aslund, Murphy, "Hawk" and L. Jones

Lt. Pat Murphy and Lcdr. Ray Hawkins

Angel In The Cockpit

Hawk Punches Out!

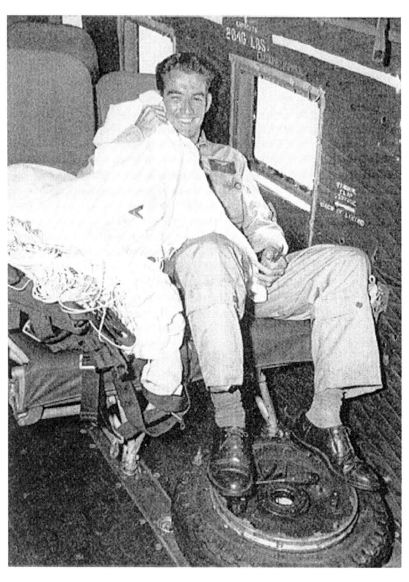

<u>On my way back to Memphis</u>

Chapter Fourteen

Test Pilot

After finishing my tour as Commanding Officer of the Blue Angels in April of 1954, I was assigned to the Weapons Test Squadron Five, VX-5, based at Naval Air Station Moffett Field, California, as a Test Pilot.

We had entered the atomic age when the Air Force dropped the atomic bombs on Japan. At this stage the Air Force, with its high altitude bombers, had the only safe means of delivering an atomic weapon. The Navy had to play catch-up if we were to play any part in what was becoming an atomic defense force.

The Navy had aircraft that could carry an atomic bomb but the problem was the requirement to accurately hit the target and then escape the blast. In Weapons Test Squadron Five, we developed a system called Low Altitude Bombing System (LABS) that would satisfy this requirement. We called it loft-bombing and we created procedures for all nuclear-capable aircraft in the Navy inventory.

The loft-bombing procedures were quite simple. You start with the selection of an initial position (IP) from photos of the ground area around the target. The IP is to be a certain distance from the target and could be a lake, a bend in a river, a prominent building or any easily discernible object. You fly over this position at a very low altitude and at a predetermined maximum speed. You pull up into a looping maneuver, holding a set "G" force on the aircraft. When you reach the correct nose up position, about a 45-degree angle, the bomb is automatically released. The bomb continues on its loft trajectory toward the target, while you continue your looping maneuver. As you pass over the top of your maneuver you roll out and dive for the deck. This puts you going safely away from the blast area at a high rate of speed as the bomb proceeds to the target and detonates.

Sometimes intelligence photographs did not give you the possibility of selecting an IP at the required distance from the target. We developed a version of the loft maneuver called "Over the Shoulder" that could be used in such a case. You fly the same maximum speed and "G" force except you pull up into your looping maneuver directly over the target. When your angle of climb is straight up, the bomb is released. It continues upward until gravity stops its climb and returns it to the target. As the bomb is in free fall, you finish your looping maneuver, roll out and dive for the deck to escape the blast

We had to develop a version of the loft maneuver for each different model of our Navy aircraft that could carry the atomic bomb. I was assigned the F7U, Cutlass. The Cutlass was a very oddly shaped aircraft. It was futuristic in appearance with its tailless swept wing design, crowned by a bulbous nose. Its tricycle landing gear, with its very high nose gear, made the Cutlass a good candidate for use in the delivery of atomic weapons. Its landing gear gave enough clearance that it could easily carry the weapon externally. The early weapons were of considerable size which made the assignment of the nicknames such as "Fat Boy" or "Fat Man", well taken.

Four test pilots were assigned to assist me in the development of the loft-bombing profile for the Cutlass. Together, we flew literally hundreds of bombing runs, calculating the proper speed, "G" force and angle of release for the bomb, to allow it maximum travel and accuracy, while giving the pilot sufficient time to escape the blast. We even flew over, around and through the clouds formed by the atomic bombs that were being test fired in the Nevada desert in the course of our experiments.

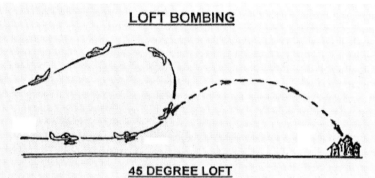

45 DEGREE LOFT
Pilot pulls up at the Initial Position (IP), Bomb is released when the aircraft is at about 45 degrees up. Bomb continues to target while the pilot completes his maneuver and escapes the blast.

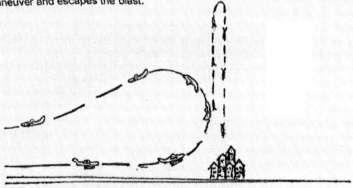

OVER THE SHOULDER LOFT
The pilot runs in and pulls up directly over the target. When the aircraft is at about a 90 degree up angle (straight up) the bomb is released. It travels up until gravity pull starts it back down and it falls on the target. While the bomb travels up the pilot completes his maneuver and escapes the blast.

It was during these test flights that I found myself faced with two incidents that would certainly lend themselves to the theory of divine intervention that has been weaving itself through the pages of this book.

One of these flights was in the Cutlass. The futuristic design of the Cutlass, with its delta shape and no tail, gave it many excellent flight characteristics. It also had some characteristics that were very bad. One such bad feature was the fact that the aircraft would not go into an inverted spin. The closest it would come to anything approaching an inverted spin was a violent sloshing maneuver going both from side to side to nose up and nose down. This maneuver became known as an auto gyration.

All aviators have been schooled in how to recover from an inverted spin but none of the same recovery techniques would work to get out of the auto gyration. After two pilots had lost their lives in accidents believed caused by the auto gyration, one of the Navy's top test pilots was assigned the task of developing a procedure to safely recover from the problem.

Two planes were assigned for the test. The test pilot flew the Cutlass and the other plane acted as chase and filmed the activities as the Cutlass was put through its paces. At somewhere around 25,000 feet the test pilot purposely put the Cutlass into an auto gyration. The film from the chase plane showed the Cutlass entering the most violent side to side and nose up and down maneuver that could be imagined. It was like a falling leaf that had changed its slow descending movements to ones so violent that it was trying to tear itself apart.

The test pilot reported by radio that he was being thrown about the cockpit with his head banging against the canopy. The chase plane continued filming the falling Cutlass. Then the test pilot stopped making reports over the radio. The film shows the Cutlass continuing its violent auto gyration all the way down. It hit the ground with complete loss of aircraft and life. For a pilot the film was horrible to watch.

I was aware of this bad habit of the Cutlass and the history of the attempts to find a recovery technique. On one of my Cutlass flights, I came face to face with the dreaded auto gyration myself, not at 25,000 feet but at around 6,000 feet.

Up to this point, I made many bomb runs in the Cutlass without any trouble. On this particular flight I arrived at the target with the intent of making eight bomb droops. On my first bombing run I ran in at full power with both afterburners cut in. At about 500 knots I pulled up over the IP into a four "G" looping maneuver. Holding the four "G's" the bomb released as the proper angle was reached. Upon reaching the top of the looping maneuver the Cutlass stalled. With a violent snap roll, the Cutlass flattened out and went into an auto gyration at about 6,000 feet.

I took every action I thought might help right the situation. I came out of after burner. I cut power. I stomped the rudders and tried every position with the stick - all to no avail. Then for some unknown reason I did something I would not normally do. I reached over and lowered the landing gear. The plane stopped its auto gyration and leveled out. As I applied power to stop any further descent, I found that one engine had flamed out due either to the auto gyration or my violent cutting of the power. As the gear was already down and the airfield was only twelve miles from the bombing target, I headed in on one engine and landed all in one piece.

Investigation showed the cause of my near accident was an improperly set gearbox that controlled the "G" force indicator and the bomb release. The "G" force indicator had been set at five "G's" instead of four. So when I pulled the needle up to the prescribed line I was pulling five "G's" all the way through the bombing run. With the high rate of speed and the excessive "G" force the Cutlass stalled as I approached the top of the looping maneuver and snapped into an auto gyration.

All was not lost though as, "All's well that ends well." We found out that throwing down your gear on the Cutlass when it is in an auto gyration will shift the center of gravity of the aircraft, which may bring the plane out of this deadly maneuver.

The other flight I flew while a test pilot in VX-5 that seems to certainly fall into the category of "Angel in the Cockpit" was flown in a Lockheed Seastar (TV-2). The Seastar was a two seated jet trainer aircraft that we used in VX-5 to train pilots in executing the loft-bombing maneuver. We also used it for data gathering flights made during the atom bomb tests in the Nevada desert. On these flights we would also test different types of flight gear to determine which would give you the best protection from radiation and glare. The TV-2 was also extensively used as a utility aircraft. I was on a utility flight from our home base at NAS Moffett Field, California, to our target ranges in China Lake, California, when a series of unusual events began to occur.

The TV-2 has two external wing tip fuel tanks, fuel tanks in each wing and a relatively small main tank in the fuselage. When the switches are all on, fuel will flow from each wing tank into the main fuselage tank to be used by the engine. On a normal flight the pilot will "gang bar" (turn on all fuel switches) as he is rolling down the runway. This will start feeding fuel to his main fuel tank. On this particular flight the maintenance crew had just put new external fuel tanks on the aircraft and they instructed me not to "gang bar" the fuel switches until I was airborne. They also asked that I only turn on the external tank switch, to check that the transfer was working properly before turning on the other switches.

All was well and good as I was on my roll for take off. After getting airborne I raised the landing gear. Immediately the plane went into a violent skid. The wheel well door on the starboard gear had closed ahead of the main gear coming up and the main gear was chattering on the door trying to get into the wheel well. Trying to correct this problem I recycled the gear several times and I put positive "G's" on the aircraft hoping to hold the wheel well door from closing first. All of this was to no avail and I notified the Moffett Field tower that I was returning to base with a mechanical problem. The tower cleared me for landing.

As I approached the field on my downwind leg, things got awful quiet as the engine ground to a halt. I had not "gang barred" the fuel switches so the thirty-five gallons in the main fuel tank was all gone, no fuel, no fire. I was too low to transfer fuel into the main fuel tank and go through a restart, so I continued my dead stick landing. I lowered my landing gear but it did not go down. The main gear had chattered so long on the wheel door that the system had overheated and shut down.

I immediately knew I would have to jettison the external fuel tanks as I did not want to slide down the runway on the belly of the aircraft with sparks flying all over that raw fuel. I jettisoned the tanks and turned in for a belly landing. At this point I could see that I did not have enough altitude to make the runway, so I decided to put it in the water. I turned north into San Francisco Bay and prepared for a water landing. I reached up and pulled the lever that should blow the canopy off.

Nothing happened. After repeated attempts the canopy did not move. I could see myself going into the water in this sealed coffin when I thought, "Oh well, see if the canopy will open normally." I reached over and hit the electric switch and up the canopy came. I felt sure it would blow off in the heavy slipstream, but no luck, she stayed right there.

I was approaching the water and tried to make a smooth landing so the canopy would not slam down and seal me in the cockpit. I greased the plane onto the water and the plane made one big bounce and came to a stop. The canopy stayed up and I hurriedly began making my exit from the aircraft.

As I stepped out on the wing I realized the plane was not sinking and water was hardly covering my shoes. Here I was, safely on top of probably the only sandbar in the middle of San Francisco Bay, and the rescue helicopter was already hovering overhead to pick me up. As they took me into Moffett Field, it was hard to believe how all this had happened.

It got even harder to believe when the "Mary Ann" (the floating crane) went out to retrieve the aircraft. Because of the sandbar the "Mary Ann" could not get up close enough to attach a hook to the aircraft. A plan was devised to float the aircraft closer, so the hookup could be made. Rubber air bags were put under the two wings and the tail of the aircraft. CO_2 bottles attached to the bags were opened. The bag under the tail of the aircraft began to inflate first and the aircraft started moving forward, After about fifty feet of travel the aircraft took a dive and submerged into about a hundred feet of water. It was realized that I had come to a stop on a narrow sandbar that was not more than a hundred feet across. The plane was recovered, had an overhaul, and was returned to service.

Well, so much for the "Angel in the Cockpit" flights. My tour in test was enjoyable and I left with a feeling of satisfaction that the test work we had done kept Naval Air a vital member of our Armed Forces, capable of delivering atomic weapons. It should be remembered that these accomplishments, when looked at in today's environment of laser and satellite guided bombs, might seem antique, but back then it was the best we had.

As I read my detaching orders, I was elated to find that after a short six- month's stint in the Pentagon, I was to assume command of Attack Squadron Forty-Six (VA-46). It is the dream of all Naval Aviators to one day command their own squadron and here I was about to embark on that dream.

Photo Album

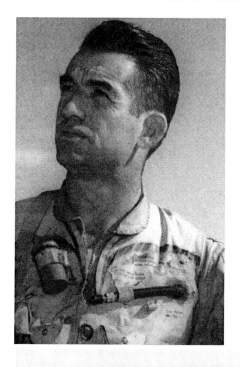

Me, as a test pilot

Any landing you can swim away from

Chapter Fifteen

Cold War

I finished my temporary duty in the Pentagon and reported into Attack Squadron Forty Six (VA-46). I did not know that I was entering into what I, today, call the cold war years of my career. In this ten-year span of time, the Navy trained, trained and trained to remain fully combat ready if war ever came. At the same time, we did everything possible to ensure that a war never came. The cold war was a tense necessity and we needed to win to thwart communism around the world.

The cold war was being fought by diplomacy from the White House and State Department, while the Department of Defense demonstrated our power by showing our flag around the world. As I've said above, we of the fleet were to remain razor sharp and ready while the cold war was being played out. It was during these cold war years that my career took many fruitful turns.

When I reported to VA-46 the squadron consisted of twenty-six officers and one-hundred-forty-eight enlisted men. The squadron was equipped with twelve F9F-8, Panther, aircraft and twelve A4D-1, Skyhawk, aircraft. My mission was to train the squadron in the A4D-1s and phase out the F9F-8s, thereby giving the Navy another squadron capable of delivering of atomic weapons.

VA-46 Insignia

The Douglas **A4D**, Skyhawk, was the Navy's first jet designed as a bomber from the ground up. It was small, light and rugged, but could carry up to 10,000 pounds of bombs. Its performance and agility were so good that the instructors at the famous "Top Gun" school at Miramar, California successfully used it to simulate enemy aircraft. Nearly three thousand were produced in its twenty-year production run and the final Skyhawks were not removed from service until the 90's. Skyhawks remain in service with many other Navies and Air Forces to this day.

The Skyhawk was a much livelier bird than the Panther and our training was intense. We finally attained that razor sharp readiness mandated. In the process, we won the Commander Fleet Air Jacksonville's yearly safety award trophy. We had flown over 2,000 hours without an accident, but as every aviator knows, once you have accepted a safety trophy, look out, the

Angel In The Cockpit

boogieman is going to bite you. Bite he did, as it could not have been more than three to four weeks after the big ceremony, accepting the trophy, that we had two quick accidents.

The first accident happened on a checkout flight for one of my young pilots in an A4D Skyhawk. I was his chase pilot. My job was to follow him through the flight, giving instruction as needed. We had finished the flight in fine fashion and returned to base for landing. As we turned onto the final leg in the landing pattern, I received a excited radio call from the young pilot saying, "Skipper, I've lost power and can't make the runway!" I directed him to maintain his air speed, select a clear area, pick up his landing gear and put "her" on the ground.

The plane hit the ground in a partially clear area short of the runway. I flew low over the downed plane to see if the pilot was having any trouble getting out of the cockpit. To my surprise there was no one in the cockpit. The canopy was missing and the seat was no longer in the cockpit. On my second pass I could see what had happened. It was clear that sometime after the plane hit the ground the pilot had ejected himself from the aircraft. The seat was laying a short distance in front of the wreck. To be there, it was obvious he had ejected as the aircraft came to a stop. I could see the pilot violently kicking to get free of the seat and unfastened from his parachute. On my next pass the pilot was up and waving to me. The crash mobile equipment, fire trucks and an ambulance, were coming off the end of the runway to pick up the downed pilot. With drying fuel tanks, I landed and taxied back to the hangar to await the return of the prodigal aviator. It's hard to believe the pilot was alive and sitting on the ground unharmed, after ejecting himself from a crashed aircraft. If this sounds miraculous, wait until I tell you of the second accident that took place a few days after this one.

The second accident happened when one of my pilots was returning from a night cross-country flight. He was flying one of the squadron's F9F-8 Panther aircraft. The pilot had radioed the tower for permission to land. With permission granted, he came in over the duty runway to make a break for landing. The pilot lowered his wheels and speed brake in preparation for touchdown. As the speed brake came down, a hydraulic leak occurred, dumping gallons of hydraulic fluid into the hot fire of the jet engine. The resulting flames lit up the night sky over the air base. The pilot continued his approach and touched down on the runway, traveling at a somewhat higher speed than that of a normal landing and it did not slow down. The airfield crash equipment had been alerted and rushed to the spot where the aircraft left the end of the runway and burst into a huge ball of fire. The crash crew feverishly fought the flames, trying to extricate the pilot. A lone figure came walking out of the darkness into the light of the flames. It was the pilot, walking down the runway toward the scene of the accident.

After successfully landing the burning aircraft on the duty runway, the pilot found himself speeding down the runway at around 120 miles per hour. With the hydraulic leak he also had no brakes. At this speed and with his aircraft engulfed in flames, he made a quick decision and ejected himself from the aircraft. With the aircraft traveling at this high speed, the pilot, still in his seat, traveled a short distance up in the air and came down on the runway behind the aircraft. The aircraft, sans pilot, sped on down the runway. Due to the darkness, no one had seen the pilot eject. With little or no injuries he was able to free himself from the seat, walk down the runway and make his appearance on the scene where the crash crew was battling the flames to save his life. Those who know about aviation and the methods of escape from a crippled jet aircraft, would be the first to tell you, "that

Angel In The Cockpit

for these young pilots to have lived through these accidents, is nothing short of miraculous." Some people would say, "Man, were those two pilots lucky." However, most of the people I know would say, "Those two pilots had an angel looking out for them." Since I was so closely associated with these two accidents I could say, "My angel must have extended his area of influence and given protection to those two young aviators."

I feel that I should say here, that over the years advances in safety devices have progressed to the point that today a pilot may safely eject himself from his airplane whether it is in the air or at a dead stop on the ground. The explosive device that fires the seat out of the airplane now has a rocket booster that will propel the pilot into the air high enough for the parachute to open.

During our training in and around Jacksonville, Florida, we frequently had made landings and takeoffs from the aircraft carrier, *Franklin D. Roosevelt* (CV-42). After my two-year tour in VA-46, I continued my ties with the *Roosevelt*, when I was ordered to duty as "Air Boss" of the ship's Air Department. Every Naval officer knows that he must get his ticket punched - serve as a Department Head of a combat vessel - if he expects to be promoted into the upper ranks. The time had arrived to get my ticket punched.

The *U.S.S. Franklin D. Roosevelt*, CV-42, was one of the new modern carriers of the Midway class, incorporating design lessons learned during World War 2. In 1954 she went through an extensive upgrade and modernization. A new, angled flight deck was installed along with steam catapults, modernized radar and advanced landing controls.

The Air Department is charged with all flight operations on and in close proximity, around the ship. During the take-off and landings the flight deck of the carrier becomes the most dangerous environment a sailor could find himself in during his entire career in the Navy. To explain a little of this environment, picture if you can, you are on the deck with forty or more aircraft, all with their engines turning up. You are there with at least sixty or seventy officers and sailors darting in, around and under these aircraft, preparing them for take-off.

Many of the aircraft are propeller driven with their huge propellers biting at the air or anything that comes near. The jet aircraft emit blasts of hot air from each tail, raising the temperature on the deck to almost unbearable. This blast is also extremely dangerous as it can blow a man down, blow him back into the pack of airplanes that are turning up, or blow him off the ship into the ocean. No matter how bad it gets on deck you have your assigned duty and you go about carrying it out. As I explain a little more about the air operations, I am sure you will see that this is not a place you would like to be.

As "Air Boss," my position during flight operations is in "Pry Fly," high up in the superstructure of the ship. I have a view of the entire flight deck, making it possible for me to direct all take-off and landings. As the ship is turned into the prevailing wind, I give the order to, "launch aircraft." At this moment a ballet in color begins.

Every officer and enlisted man on the flight deck is wearing a colored jersey that designates the job that he is performing. Those with the yellow jerseys are charged with all movement of aircraft about the deck. The blue shirts are the chock men and plane pushers. Following the yellow jersey's direction, the blue jerseys have pushed the planes into their present positions and are now all underneath the aircraft. They are awaiting the signal from the yellow shirts to remove the chocks so the aircraft can be moved forward.

Following the yellow jersey's signals the pilot taxies the aircraft forward to a spot on the catapult. Here the catapult crew (green jerseys) secures the aircraft to the catapult and signals to the launching officer that the catapult is ready. The launching officer motions to the pilot for a full throttle turn up. With a salute from the pilot, indicating he is ready for launch, the launching officer reaches forward, touches the deck and the catapult fires, sending the aircraft into the air. This ballet continues with an airplane being launched about every twenty seconds, until all planes, scheduled for launch, are in the air.

With the launch completed the ballet continues as the deck is made ready for the flight waiting to land. The landing cycle brings out many different colored jerseys that will blend with those colors most prevalent during the take-off cycle.

The yellow, blue and green jerseys, as in the take-off cycle, control all movement of the aircraft on the deck during the landing cycle. The green jerseys will set and control the arresting gear, which the pilot will catch upon landing. A required setting will be entered into the gear, stressing the arresting cables to correspond with the weight of each aircraft, as it enters the groove for landing. As the plane catches the arresting cable, the yellow jersey will start giving the pilot signals to raise the tail hook and fold the plane's wings. Then he is directed forward to the bow, where the engine is shut down. The blue jerseys push the plane into a tight spot and secure the plane to the deck with chain tie-downs.

It is here that the other colored jerseys start to appear. The brown jerseys of the plane captains are seen as they follow their planes moving up the deck. The plane captains will assist the pilots in exiting the cockpits and start readying their planes for the next launch. The purple jersey gas gang will swarm over the aircraft to refuel the aircraft as quickly as possible. You will see the red jersey ordnance crews rearming or unloading ordnance from the aircraft, as may be required. Also, always on ready standby for any medical alert that may be required, are the hospital corpsmen, with their white jerseys sporting a big red cross on the front and back.

Over my eighteen-month tour as Air Boss, I must have watched this colorful ballet play out over a thousand times. Every time I watched, I gained more and more respect for those young troops down on the deck, who fearlessly faced danger every day. Just to give you a feel of how dangerous it can be, I will relate the story of a devastating deck accident that happened during a launching cycle.

We had an F8 Crusader turning up at full power on the catapult, awaiting the signal for launch. The "catapult leading" chief saw something that was not right and without thinking, crossed in front of the aircraft. The tremendous suction created by the jet engine of the aircraft at full power pulled the chief into the air intake of the aircraft. The plane was shut down as quickly as possible and the chief barely hanging onto life, was removed from the engine nacelle. He was flown off the ship to a hospital on shore but I hate to report he failed to recover from the ordeal.

As I continued my eighteen-month tour as head of the Air Department I certainly learned why it was so important to have had such an assignment when being considered for promotion. You learned the internal working of a combat vessel, the importance of close teamwork between the many departments to insure the smooth operation of the ship, plus the important leadership qualities required in command of the men assigned to your charge.

Angel In The Cockpit

Following my tours as Commanding Officer of Attack Squadron 46, and as "Air Boss" of the Air Department of the *Franklin D. Roosevelt*, I received orders as the Commander of Carrier air group One. The air group consisted of six fighter and attack squadrons containing 100 aircraft and somewhat over 1,000 personnel. air group One was the *Roosevelt's* assigned air group so this would mean I would be starting my fourth and fifth year in a row, attached to the *Roosevelt*.

When I brought air group One aboard, the *Roosevelt*, with it's massive capabilities, was transformed into a first line combatant warship. The air group is literally the main offensive and defensive battery of the carrier and fulfills the ship's purpose. The construction, design and characteristics of the air group and the *Roosevelt* demand that they be melded into an integral unit, since neither could survive without the other.

With my past assignments on the *Roosevelt,* it was an easy task to mold the air group into a close knit, smooth working unit with the other departments of the ship. The *Roosevelt* was then, one of the larger carriers in the fleet, having an angle deck, steam catapults and other capabilities to operate heavier aircraft. air group One brought five of its six squadrons to the *Roosevelt*. The composition was two fighter and three attack squadrons. One of the attack squadrons was Heavy Attack Squadron 11, equipped with twelve A3D Skywarriors. The Skywarrior was a twin engine jet aircraft, fully capable of high altitude delivery of the atomic weapon. The *Roosevelt*, with this improved and very visible atomic bomb delivery capability, continued to be the "darling" of all the capital ships of our Navy, carrying out the cold war.

The *Roosevelt*, along with our other capital ships, have steamed thousand upon thousands of miles to friendly countries of the world, showing our flag and spreading friendship. In this manner, we have assured our allies that our power and capabilities lie not only in our ability to enforce peace, but also to serve mankind in many other humane ways. Our mighty warships have written proof in history that peace can be preserved, and a powerful nation need not be an aggressor in anything but to accomplish that end.

As I completed my five year association with the *Franklin D. Roosevelt,* I could look back on three enjoyable tours serving in positions that are an aviator's dream - that of Commanding Officer of a Squadron, "Air Boss" and as the Commander of an air group. These tours went smoothly for me, and the knowledge I gained was something that would serve me well all my life. In these five years the *Roosevelt* made five, six-month deployments to the Mediterranean Sea, where we made many ports of call showing the flag and demonstrating our combat power. It was at one of these port calls I received orders: upon return to the States, I would be detached from duty as Commander, Carrier air group One and would report for duty in the Pentagon. During flight operations before my departure, I had the distinct pleasure of making the 100,000th carrier landing registered on the *Roosevelt's* deck. It was with the memory of the ceremony of cutting the cake for this landing that I made my departure from the *Roosevelt* and sadly said goodbye to my officers and men of air group One. With orders in hand, I took my leave and headed for my assignment in the Pentagon.

Photo Album

Commander Hawkins receives the Safety Award from the Admiral.

The U.S.S. Franklin D. Roosevelt, CV-42

L to R: CAG, Commander Fair, Air Boss, Commander Hawkins and Asst. Air Boss Commander Topliff.

Angel In The Cockpit

100,000th Landing Celebration

Chapter Sixteen

Deep Draft Command

When I arrived at the Pentagon, I was informed that I would be assigned to the office of the Assistant Chief of Naval Operations (General Planning and Programming). I had gotten in a few days before I was to report for duty. I decided I would visit the Bureau of Naval Personnel and talk with the person who assigned me to this detail to find out why I was being put in program planning instead of on the aviation side of the house.

I was told that the Secretary of Defense had directed that a Five-Year Defense Plan (FYDP) would be put together and that all future budget requests would be predicated on this plan. The office of General Planning and Programming (OP-90) was to be the coordinating office for the development of this plan for the Navy Department. Since this office had no aviation officers assigned, it was decided to bring in two senior aviation officers to ensure that aviation interests were put forth and considered. I was to be one of these officers.

Satisfied as to the reason for my duty assignment, I reported aboard and became one of the first naval aviators to be assigned to the Office of General Planning and Programming. For someone who had eluded assignment of a full tour of duty in the Pentagon for twenty-three years, I was about to enter into another world.

We immersed ourselves into the development of the Five Year Defense Plan, not realizing that it would be a massive effort spanning many months before completion and approval. Secretary McNamara and his staff of "Whiz Kids" were attempting to manage the Department by making the decisions on all subjects, down to the minute details. This type of management kept the Pentagon staff on fifteen to eighteen hour workdays and six to seven day workweeks. The Secretary's normal workday was from six in the morning until six or seven at night. When he left at night he would pass to the Secretaries of the Military Departments a list of questions. He wanted the answers on his desk when he came in the next morning.

In the case of the Navy Secretary, he would pass the questions to be answered by the Navy Department to our office, OP-90, and we would farm them out through the Department for answers. After coordinating the return of all answers we would funnel them back through the Navy Secretary, who would get them to Secretary McNamara's office before he arrived in the morning.

This went on day after day and you can see why the long work hours were inescapable. No one could go home until Secretary McNamara left the office and the requested information filtered down to the people who would furnish the required answers for the next morning. Depending on the information requested, many offices could be required to fully staff the report. Many times the whole Navy Department would be tied up to put together the required information requested in the report. In peak budget times and other times of stress, these long days carried over into the weekends.

Secretary McNamara was a speed-reader, requiring all reports to be on a normal 8.5" by 11" page. He could absorb the information as fast as he could turn the page and had the capability to retain mounds of information. Any expert manager will tell you that too much information can sometimes be bad. You can become saturated with minute details and miss the big decisions that need to be made. There comes a time when subordinates have to be given authority to carry out your directives, keeping your mind clear for other higher decisions. Secretary McNamara often forgot the importance of delegation.

One incident from the Cuban Missile Crisis sticks in my mind. Secretary McNamara was in the Combat Control Center in the Pentagon. This is a huge set of rooms down in the bowels of the building where the commanders can communicate with all of our worldwide forces. The Secretary seized a radio microphone and began directing a destroyer skipper how to operate his ship.

I could go on about the good things and the bad things I observed of McNamara and his "Whiz Kids" staff. But I will save that until a later chapter, when I cover my second Pentagon tour.

You would think that this fast pace, day after day, would burn anyone out, but you get used to it and you know you are not alone. Your fellow officers and enlisted men have to endure the same long workdays and weekends. It's a bit hard on the family life, but still better than sea duty, where you are totally away from the family for long stretches at a time. Whatever the hardship, you stick with it and carry out your assigned duty.

This we did, and after a long bout of detail planning we developed a Five Year Defense Plan that we were proud of and one that received the praise of Secretary McNamara and the Assistant Secretary of Defense (Comptroller). With this five-year plan we could go about submitting our October yearly budget.

The plan was a great tool for backing up our budget submission. For instance, if the plan showed that new ships were to come into the force within the five years of the plan

- then it was time to get the funds into the budget. Most major shipbuilding takes five years or longer. My entire tour in the Pentagon was spent in that other world I mentioned earlier. This was a world where all discussions or presentations of budget requests were spoken in billions of dollars not millions.

Surviving two years in this high-flying surrounding, I lucked out with a set of orders that would put me in a year of study at the Navy War College in Newport, Rhode Island. The War College is a place where senior officers are assigned, without giving them any specific duty requirements. They are to rest, relax, attend high level seminars, engage in computer war games and study. Each officer attending writes a thesis on some lofty subject that should better the Navy or Marine Corps in its operations, administration, weaponry, battle plans, etc. It was my luck to arrive at a time when the assigned Commandant of the War Collage did not believe in this business about rest and relaxation. Not only did we do all those things I listed above, but, to further enhance our minds, he also had us signing up for after-hours study at George Washington University.

All in all, the months of study at the War College were a fruitful tour. We had a chance to get away from the demands of the day-to-day operations, giving us a chance to study the overall Navy and what we thought it should look like in the future. We had the privilege of hearing from leaders of not only the military services but also, from the corporate world.

Our war gaming was done in teams, so that different solutions could be observed for the military problem being gamed. Many of the games were pointed to study the use of atomic weapons in total war, as well as, in a limited war. I must say that we learned a lot of how, and how not, to use such weapons from the games of the entire class.

Angel In The Cockpit

The months of study came to an end much too soon but, as it ended, I did receive some exceptional news. The Deep Draft Board had met and I had been selected to receive an assignment as Commanding Officer of one of the supply ships in the Navy. What this meant to me was that this was one more step toward getting an assignment as Commanding Officer of one of the aircraft carriers of our fleet. The thought was that since the aviation officers had not been schooled in the operations of a naval vessel, they should be assigned to command of one of our large supply ships. This would allow them to learn the ins and outs of the operation of a deep draft vessel before being assigned to command of one of our aircraft carriers.

I received my orders as Commanding Officer of the *USS Caloosahatchee* (AO-98), a fleet oiler, whose mission was the underway replenishment of the fleet with the delivery of bunker oil, aviation gasoline and JP-5 jet fuel. The *Caloosahatchee* was based at the Newport, Road Island harbor and was a member of Service Squadron Two (SERVRON-TWO) with headquarters in Norfolk, Virginia. I spent a week at SERVRON-TWO, where I paid my respects, brushed up on the maritime rules of the road and reviewed the squadron operating procedures. I then returned to Newport, and at a change of command ceremony on 14 July 1965, I received command of the USS *Caloosahatchee*.

Being based in Newport was a boon for me. By being away from the squadron headquarters in Norfolk, I was able to set my own training schedule and Newport was so situated that you could have the ship down the channel and out into the open sea in a matter of thirty to forty minutes. Also there was an aircraft carrier based nearby, at Quonset Point, Rhode Island, which made it convenient to meet and practice underway replenishment with another combat ship.

The **USS** *Caloosahatchee* (**AO-98**) was launched at the very end of World War Two and entered service just after the war's end. At 35,000 tons, she was bigger than the carriers "Hawk served on during the Pacific Campaigns. The *Caloosahatchee* served with the Navy for 45 years before being retired in 1990.

We made training sorties down the channel every chance we got, both day and night. I must say that the duty I had done earlier in my career, on the *USS Portsmouth*, where I had qualified and functioned as Officer of the Deck, made my training on the *Caloosahatchee* much easier.

It was on one of these training sorties that we were working with the aircraft carrier from Quonset Point that we had our first near disaster. The carrier had come alongside, a hook-up for the transfer of aviation fuel had been accomplished and the transfer of fuel was underway. About thirty minutes into the operation, the carrier suddenly started a turn to starboard, away from us.

Angel In The Cockpit

I tried to follow by speeding up and matching the turn, but the turn was too great. The hoses and lines started snapping. My First Lieutenant saw what was about to happen and cut off the flow of gasoline and ordered our crew to take cover. Luckily no one was injured and the gasoline flow had been stopped in time, so no fire broke out.

The captain of the aircraft carrier came up on the radio explaining that his helmsman had been relieved during the exercise and the helmsman who had come on duty received an incorrect heading causing the sharp turn to starboard. He said that his supply officer would be over when we returned to port to make restitution for our busted hoses and broken cables. True to form, the supply officer arrived with requisition slips for every item we had reported broken. I think the aircraft carrier skipper did not want this little snafu to get on his record.

After initial training we went through an inspection from the SERVRON--TWO staff and were declared ready to service the fleet. We fulfilled many requests for service from ships transiting the Atlantic and by those training in the Newport area. We made one deployment to the Mediterranean, where we serviced the ships in the Sixth Fleet. All this was done without a single mishap.

There was one assignment that had nothing to do with the replenishment function that gave me much pleasure. The *Caloosahatchee* was to cover the secondary location of the landing of the *Gemini 8* spacecraft. The primary landing location was somewhere in the middle of the Atlantic Ocean and the secondary location was off the West Coast of Africa, a few hundred miles from Dakar. Any deviation of up to one degree on the reentry angle would see the capsule landing somewhere in the secondary location. I was given command of four destroyers, and they joined the *Caloosahatchee* in a loose formation, as we proceeded to our assigned recovery location.

We arrived on station a day and a half before scheduled splashdown. I released the destroyers to remain in the area directing them to conduct any training they deemed appropriate. We kept radio contact with the astronauts as they passed overhead. As splashdown approached, I spread the destroyers around in the area to give us the best chance to spot the reentry if it developed in our area. Because of weather, and some unknown problem with the capsule, the landing in the Atlantic was scrubbed and the landing was made in the Pacific Ocean. When I received this message, I directed the unit to reform and we would proceed to our homeport.

As we headed for home a message was received from SERVRON TWO stating that a distress call had been received from a Norwegian merchant ship on its way from Rio de Janeiro to Dakar. We were told that the ship reported being on fire, dead in the water and needing assistance from any ship in the area. I was told that the *Caloosahatchee* was the nearest ship and should proceed and offer any assistance feasible.

I was given the position of the distressed ship and could tell it would take at least two days for the *Caloosahatchee*, traveling at top speed to arrive on the scene. I directed one of the destroyers, the *USS Myles C. Fox*, to proceed at top speed and to offer what assistance he could give them while awaiting our arrival the next day. I released two of the destroyers and told them to return to their homeport. The other destroyer, the *USS Charles P. Cecil*, who was on his way from a far corner of the recovery area, was told to proceed to the distress scene at normal cruising speed. I cranked up *Caloosahatchee's* top speed of thirteen knots and headed for the distressed ship.

Angel In The Cockpit

We arrived about 10:30 in the morning and observed a merchant ship with smoke bellowing out of one of the cargo holds. I received a report from the *Fox* skipper, who had arrived on the scene a day earlier. He reported that he had put a boat in the water and sent a small crew over to the distressed vessel. The captain of the merchant ship had requested assistance from the *Fox* crew to put out the fire. As for the merchant ship's crew, the *Fox* skipper reported that the best he could find out was that the crew was not doing much of anything but wanting to get off the ship. He said that he told the Captain that we were coming in the *Caloosahatchee* and that we had much more capacity to offer assistance.

We put a boat in the water and my Executive Officer and six of our crew boarded the distressed ship to survey the situation and report. The Executive Officer reported that the ship had power, but that they had come to a stop because the wind was blowing into the cargo hold and fanning the flames. He reported that the cargo hold was filled with loose coffee beans in the bottom. The coffee was then covered by bales of wool almost to the top of the cargo hold. The coffee beans were on fire and his assessment was that the bales of wool had to be removed and tossed overboard. This would make room to get to the coffee beans so they could be soaked with water to extinguish the smoldering fire. He also reported that of the ten or so electric cranes only two were working and that the ship's crew was sitting on their duffs and seemed to be waiting to leave the ship.

I made a trip over to talk personally with the Captain. I told him that we could help him save his ship, but we would have to jettison some of the cargo. He admitted he was the Captain of the ship but there was also another captain aboard, who was Captain of the cargo, and he was adamant that the cargo not be thrown overboard. I told him I did not understand why the cargo captain was so against it because if we did not do it he would loose his entire cargo and have a call on his insurance. If we jettisoned some of his cargo, he would still have an insurance call on that which was lost. I again told the Captain that it was his ship and the decision was his to make.

His decision was swift. He said, "Your offer of assistance is accepted, please do whatever is necessary to put out the flames." I returned to the *Caloosahatchee* and told the Executive Officer his plan had been accepted and directed him to proceed with its execution.

The Executive Officer and several members from our crew returned to the distressed ship. Our electrician had four of the electric cranes operating in less than an hour and things were ready to start jettisoning the bales of wool. Our leading chief took charge of the distressed ship's wayward crew and got them off their duffs and joined up as a team to assist in the removal of the bales. The wool started coming up out of the cargo hole as fast as the cranes could snatch it out. As the bales went over the side they started floating away and could be seen for miles behind the ship. As the last bale came out a red hot mass was visible, buried deep in the mound of coffee beans that filled the bottom of the cargo hold. It was obvious that it would have been only a short time before the bales of wool would have ignited, taking the ship to the bottom. Fire hoses were used for the rest of the night to soak the coffee beans until there was no sign of fire. We stood by the next morning to watch the ship get up power and head for Dakar.

As we headed for home I started receiving personal messages from my Squadron Commander in Norfolk, He informed me that I was wanted back at the Pentagon and he thought orders were being written for me to report when I returned to Newport. Well, here we were miles from Newport and I had no idea what was going on and no way to get in touch with someone who could enlighten me. I was looking forward to an eighteen month tour on the *Caloosahatchee* and I had completed less than ten months. It was a long ride of considerable speculation before reaching Newport.

When I reached Newport, I found that the rumor was true. Orders lay on my desk directing me to report to the Office of the Chief of Naval Operations in the Pentagon. The mystery of why I was being relieved early from my Deep Draft Command deepened, as the orders gave me only eighteen days before reporting. I began to think that I must have done something very wrong and they were getting me back to nail me to the cross.

With the few days remaining before having to report to my new assignment, I made all my required reports on the botched planned *Gemini 8* spacecraft landing and a detailed report on the *Caloosahatchee's* assistance given to the merchant ship which had made the distress call. The Bureau of Naval Personnel had pulled a Navy Captain, from his studies at the Naval War College, as my relief and somehow we managed to get a change of command set up.

The day of the Change of Command arrived and everything went off without a hitch. My relief made his, "I am glad to be aboard," speech and I said my good-byes and thanked the crew for a job well done. The pomp and tradition of a Change of Command ceremony can bring a lump to one's throat, and I am afraid at this one there was a hint of tears in my eyes as I saluted the flag and departed the *Caloosahatchee*.

Angel In The Cockpit

Photo Album

Captain Hawkins conducts an inspection

*Farewell to the **Caloosahatchee***

Chapter Seventeen

Japan and Vietnam

With some apprehension, I reported into the Office of the Chief of Naval Operations and was told that I would be assigned to the Office of the Assistant Chief of Naval Operations, General Planning and Programming (OP-90), where I would assume the Directorship of the Program Appraisal Division (OP-90E). When I asked if anyone knew why I was pulled from the command of my Deep Draft before my tour was completed, the answer removed a lot of weight from my shoulders. I learned it was not done because of some misdeed.

The Admiral in charge of OP-90 during the time of my first Pentagon tour had received his third star – up to Vice Admiral. He had taken over the newly established position as Deputy Chief of Naval Operations, Program Planning (OP-090) and had requested me to be returned to serve on two very time sensitive studies.

The Admiral told me that because of my close association with the original development of the Five-Year Defense Plan (FYDP). He wanted me on the studies to ensure that all planning requirements were fully considered. The Admiral also said that this was the year to revise the FYDP and, as Director of the Program Appraisal Division, it would be my job to coordinate the updates. With my past knowledge of the detail workings of the FYDP, he expected the update to go smoothly.

We completed both projects over the next several months. The outcome of the larger of the two studies saw the establishment of the Naval Material Command, which was to become the umbrella command over the various Bureaus, such as the Bureau of Aeronautics, the Bureau of Ships, etc. On the other important study, the Navy Damage Limiting Study, my Program Appraisal Division (OP-90E) was instrumental in the detailed cost analysis of the various weapons systems in the study.

With the studies completed our number one priority became the update of the Five-Year Defense Plan. Along with this update our office was in daily confrontation with McNamara's "Whiz Kids" in trying to maintain a budget, and a supplement when needed, to fight the war in Vietnam.

The Vietnam War had been going on much too long already. The North Vietnamese Communists began their goal of unifying Vietnam in early 1960, upon completion of the Ho Chi Minh Trail through southern Laos and into the mountains of South Vietnam. It was through this land route and by sea that they transported arms and supplies to the Communist Viet Cong guerrillas in South Vietnam and began an armed struggle to overthrow the government of the Republic of Vietnam.

In the beginning, the United States had not done much to help the Republic of Vietnam except to furnish their Navy with some fast patrol boats and train their crews. This was the case up until the famous Tonkin Gulf incidents of August, 1964. The first incident was brought about by the attack of three Communist motor torpedo boats on the *USS Maddox*.

The U.S. destroyer was on an electronic intelligence gathering patrol, outside the territorial waters of North Vietnam.

Angel In The Cockpit

The boats fired torpedoes at the *Maddox,* but luckily they all missed. A few rounds fired by one of the boats' deck guns did strike the *Maddox.* Navy aircraft, sent from a nearby aircraft carrier to assist the *Maddox,* shot up the attackers and left one boat dead in the water.

President Johnson and Secretary of Defense McNamara decided that we could not retreat from our position of intelligence gathering on the open seas. The *Maddox* was reinforced by the destroyer *USS Turner Joy* and sent back into the Tonkin Gulf to continue its surveillance mission.

Only two days after the first attack, on the night of 4 August, the *Maddox* and *Turner Joy* made contact with several fast craft. The incident occurred far at sea in international waters. Upon receiving this word, President Johnson ordered the Seventh Fleet to initiate a strike against North Vietnam. This strike took place on 5 August 1964. Carrier planes hit fuel storage in the town of Vinh and destroyed thirty or more enemy vessels along the coast. Following this strike the U.S. Congress passed "The Tonkin Gulf Resolution", which gave President Johnson the authority to use military force, as he saw fit, against the Vietnamese Communists. By this action, the United States entered into a war that would drag on for the next ten years and I was facing the third war of my military career.

The war in Vietnam began in earnest for the United States in March of 1965. The aircraft carriers of the Seventh Fleet, operating as Task Force 77, had the major role in the bombing mission against the North Vietnamese. The carriers, and their supporting vessels, operated at "Yankee Station," in the Tonkin Gulf, and at "Dixie Station," southeast of Cam Ranh Bay. The carrier aircraft for the next two years flew campaign after campaign with high sounding names like, "Rolling Thunder," "Linebacker," etc. These strikes wreaked devastating damage on enemy power plants, fuel storage, munitions supplies, highway and railway bridges, and truck and train rolling stock. As our ground forces were inserted into South Vietnam, ground support flights became an important part of Task Force 77's mission.

As I stated above, our office was in daily confrontation with McNamara's "Whiz Kids" fighting the budget process for more money for the Navy to fight the war in Vietnam. This was not an easy task, as McNamara had brought his "Whiz Kids" into his administration to reorganize the Defense Department and clean up all, so called, waste and mismanagement, while maintaining a lean budget. Their slogan, as we approached the support of this war, was, "A Bigger Bang for the Buck." Let me say here that these gentlemen were all well educated and very intelligent. However, what they knew about the military and its operation was very sketchy to nil. This being the case, some decisions they made were unsound and some were downright comical. As a case in point, I will discuss one of these decisions. There were many others as this war was micromanaged from Washington, DC.

That decision by the "Whiz Kids" came about as a result of the Navy's request to activate two of our mothballed battleships. These battleships were to be used to hit coastal targets such as bridges, radar sites, rail lines, troop concentrations and gun positions. This same tactic had been used successfully in the Korean War, when two mothballed battleships were activated and used with good results. Following their slogan, "A Bigger Bang for the Buck," the "Whiz Kids" had to study the Navy's request and determine how the battleships could be activated and operated at the cheapest cost possible.

When the study came to the manning of the battleships, the size of the crew was stripped to the barest essentials. When asked why the number of crewmen manning the five inch guns had been cut in half, the 'Whiz Kid's" reasoning was this - they had determined that to do shore bombardment the battleship would be cruising up and down the coast to reach the assigned targets. This being the case, when the battleship was making its firing run, all the five inch guns on the starboard side of the ship could fire on the assigned targets. When the battleship made its turn to come back up the cost, all the five inch gun crews on the starboard side could vacate their guns and scurry across the deck and man the guns on the port side and take on the assigned targets from that side.

Needless to say, after a thorough briefing on the operation of a combat vessel in a hostile environment, the "Whiz Kids" relented and the battleships went into combat with their five-inch guns fully manned. Those doing the study, just were not aware of the requirements of the battle condition, "General Quarters," which is set when combat conditions are prevalent. It was explained to them that at "General Quarters," condition "Zebra" is set. All "Zebra" hatches (boldly painted with black and white stripes) must be secured, making each compartment of the ship watertight. This action also mandates that no "Zebra" hatch will be broken during "General Quarters," thereby curtailing movement about the ship.

This type of banter went on day in and day out while I was awaiting an assignment to sea duty. Having had my deep draft assignment on the *Caloosahatchee,* I was in hopes of getting a Major Command assignment - Commanding Officer of one of the aircraft carriers in Task Force 77, fighting the war in Vietnam. This was not to be though. The Major Command Board met in late 1967 and I did not receive assignment to one of the five slots open in the twelve aircraft carriers we had in the fleet at the time. I was lucky enough to receive my Major Command assignment as Commanding Officer of the Master Jet Base in

Atsugi, Japan. This would not put me in the front line action but would give me a chance to be of direct assistance to our ships on "Yankee Station," as well as, the aviation units in country. Atsugi, under the Commander, Fleet Air Western Pacific, acted as a rear training/staging area and repair facility for the aviation units operating from the carriers on "Yankee Station" and the Marine Corps units in country.

Upon my arrival in Japan, I was met by my interrupter, Sanota San, Hawaiian-born Japanese, whose first words to me were, "Captain, I am sure happy to see your gray hair. The Japanese equate age to knowledge, so you should do well." Sanota would prove his worth time after time, as he became my right hand in forging relationships with the Japanese people.

As Commanding Officer of Atsugi, I could easily see that the mission of the base was twofold. First, giving support to our war effort and second, maintaining good relations with the government and people of Japan. The first part of the mission, which was supporting the war effort, was done very well for the two years of my tour. Our most important function was the repair and maintenance of damaged and shot-up aircraft we received from the war zone. Within the confines of Atsugi, we housed the Nippon Aircraft Company (Nippi). Nippi's reputation for the restoration of aircraft was beyond reproach. They operated under the slogan, "If you send us a part of an aircraft that contains the Bureau Number, we will repair and return to you a new aircraft with the same bureau number."

We would receive these damaged or shot-up aircraft by boat, by large crane helicopters, by large transport aircraft or in some cases they would be flown in. Atsugi's Aircraft Maintenance Department (AMD) would remove the aircraft engines and confidential equipment and send the airframe to Nippi. After the airframe was repaired our AMD would replace the overhauled engine and confidential equipment, test fly the aircraft and return it to the unit in country or to the aircraft carrier. This procedure was going on all the time and on many occasions we would receive as many as three or more damaged or shot-up aircraft per day. Nippi certainly lived up to its reputation. On one occasion we delivered three helicopters to them, which had been blown into many pieces. They were able to come up with one shiny new bird by using all the pieces from the three.

The three aircraft squadrons flying out of Atsugi accomplished our other support of the war effort. These squadrons consisted of VQ-1, HC-7 and VRC-50, all under the control of Commander, Fleet Air Western Pacific, a tenant on Atsugi. VQ-1 flew over and around the war zone and the Western Pacific, gathering radar and telecommunications intelligence information. HC-7, a helicopter squadron on call for search and rescue, also had helicopter detachments on combat ships, as well as land based in the war zone. VRC-50, a carrier on board delivery squadron (COD) serviced the aircraft carriers on "Yankee Station" by the delivery of mail, emergency spare parts and personnel. The personnel could be those reporting for duty or those going or returning from emergency leave. Atsugi also became the home base of the air groups that flew off of the carriers when they had to come in to Japan from "Yankee Station" and go into Sasebo or Yokohama for repairs.

The other part of my mission, that of fostering relations with the people of Japan, was of great importance. The maintenance of our bases in this part of the world was vital to our national interest and could only be attained by the good relationship with the government and the people. To this end, I was fortunate enough to establish a friendship with the Mayor of Yamato City, the city in which Atsugi was located, the Mayor of Ayase Town, bordering Atsugi, and the Governor of Kanagawa Prefecture, the Prefecture in which Atsugi was located. Working with these fine gentlemen made my tour in Japan one of considerable satisfaction. It was great learning and observing the customs of the Japanese people.

There is one custom that I am reminded of every day as I pass by a certain painting hanging in my living room. The story of this painting came about when a letter came to me, as the Commanding Officer of Atsugi, from a person in Miami, Florida. The letter stated that during World War II, this person had acquired a samurai sword while doing duty in Japan. It also stated that he had since learned the importance of these swords to a Japanese family and he was sending the sword to me to see if I could find the rightful owner and return the sword.

The sword arrived, and with the name of the swordsmith and a serial number, we were able to locate the family that had owned the sword. This was not too hard a task as these samurai swords are all registered in Japan. We made an appointment with the family to return the sword to them. When we arrived, the entire family was gathered in a room containing a small area that looked like a religious shrine. In the middle of this shrine stood a wooden cradle on which the sword had originally sat. The father took the sword, bowed and with deep reverence placed the sword into its cradle. The father turned, bowed again and asked us to share tea. While we were having tea, I made a remark about a painting on the wall and how beautiful it was. After finishing our tea, we begged our departure and moved to our car to return to Atsugi. As I slid into the back, there on the seat was the painting that I had just admired.

I told Sanota, my interrupter, that there was no way I could accept such a gift. He assured me that there was no way I could refuse it, because if I did the father who made the gift would loose face. Needless to say, I was honor bound to accept the gift and, as I said, I think of this Japanese custom every time I view this lovely painting. I would say here, to anyone visiting a Japanese home, be careful of what you admire. You could end up with it as a gift.

My two years of duty at Atsugi came to an end, and I departed with the feeling that we had accomplished our mission of support for the war effort. It was a fruitful and safe task - only once in those two years did I come under actual fire. That was on one of my trips into the war zone. The airstrip, on Da Nang where we landed, came under heavy rocket attack by the Viet Cong. It was out of the airplane and into the nearest friendly foxhole.

I returned to the States, and what I observed was hard to believe. The "Flower Children" of the sixties were in the streets demonstrating against the war. The American flag was being burned in demonstrations all around the country. The liberal universities were banning all ROTC programs from their campuses. The media was having a field day with nothing in support for the war effort, but always daily three inch bold headlines of the body bag count and conflicting stories of how our troops were killing civilians. Young men, draft dodgers, were defecting to Canada in large numbers. Worst of all our returning veterans were being spit upon by some members of our society who had forgotten that the liberty they were enjoying was bought by the dead bodies of the many veterans who had given their lives in service to their country.

Looking at these unpatriotic happenings today, it becomes even more impossible to believe the fallout. A well-known movie actress went to North Vietnam and gave support and comfort to our enemies, causing extra hardships on our POW's, when they refused to meet with her. She came home and continued her starring rolls with no more than a whimper from the populace.

An elected Commander-in-Chief of the Armed Services gave pardons to the "draft dodgers" and welcomed them back to the United States, even though he was a Naval Academy graduate and had seen active service in the Navy. And harder yet to believe is that a Rhodes Scholar, who joined the "Love Children" in their demonstrations against the war, went to England where he spoke against his country. Even though he showed disdain for the military in his writings, he was later elected as Commander-in-Chief of that same military.

Another thing that had changed upon my return to the states was that the Johnson Administration had left office and the Nixon Administration was at the helm. It was under this administration that the character of the war changed from one of "status quo" to one of action to end this war and bring our troops home.

The North Vietnam Communists were being able to continue the war by bringing supplies into Cambodia and North Vietnam with the use of neutral merchant ships. The Seventh Fleet could have stopped this flow of goods long ago, but President Johnson prohibited such a blockade for fear of open Soviet and Chinese intervention. President Nixon on the other hand, in an attempt to end the war, ordered the Seventh Fleet to mine the waters and blockade the ports of North Vietnam. With the blockade in place the supplies to North Vietnam quickly dried up. With this and an increased bombing campaign on its major cities, the North Vietnamese agreed to a reasonable cease-fire and an agreement to release all American Prisoners of War.

President Nixon ordered our troops out of Vietnam, and the POWs began arriving back in the States. In my assignment as Director of Community Relations, in the office of the Deputy Secretary of Defense for Public Affairs, I was assistant to General "Chappie" James, the Military Assistant Secretary of Defense for Public Affairs. He was given the task of overseeing the return of the POW's to the United States. This was a heartwarming assignment, working with the wives and relatives of the POWs, ensuring that their reunions went off without a hitch. There was plenty of sadness also in the cases of those individuals who were listed as missing in action and did not show up with the returning POWs. It was during this assignment that my military career came to an end, and in June of 1973, I retired from the Navy after thirty-one years of service.

Those thirty-one years were full of enjoyment, sadness, learning and accomplishment. The enjoyment came from the many and varied assignments and the outstanding individuals I was privileged to serve with. The sadness came from the loss of my comrades and shipmates, whether it came in day-to-day routine or in combat. Learning in the Navy is continuous, it matters not what rank you attain, there is always one more lecture, school or institute of learning that you are required to attend to prepare yourself for the responsibility of your next assignment.

Accomplishment of the many tasks assigned gave me a feeling of pride. Pride not only in myself, but also pride for the Navy for which I love. If ever asked, "Would you do it all over again"? My reply, in a heart beat, would be a resounding, "Yes".

Photo Album

Captain Hawkins at the Pentagon.

I receive the Third Order of the Sacred Treasury, the first time that the Emperor had given this award to a non-Japanese.

Angel In The Cockpit

Not all Pentagon duties were onerous.

My Retirement Photo

Chapter Eighteen

Retirement

I entered retirement looking for those long hours of boredom that everyone had been telling me retirement would bring. This was not to be for me. As fate would have it, I joined the Naval Aviation Museum Foundation as its Secretary-Treasurer. I then embarked on the Foundation's mission to construct and support the operations of a Naval Aviation Museum that would be second to none. Little did I realize that I would be a part of this endeavor for the next twenty-five years.

When I came aboard the Foundation, the Naval Aviation Museum consisted of a small World War II building located on the Naval Air Station in Pensacola, Florida. It had two aircraft on display outside and a smattering of memorabilia on display inside the building.

It was in 1974 that the Foundation started construction on the first phase of a five-stage planned museum on thirty-five prime acres on the Pensacola Naval Air Station. Through the years, the Foundation received donations from the State, County, organizations, corporations and individuals. By 1998, the Foundation was able to complete four phases of the plan. The museum at that time exceeded 300,000 square feet. It boasted a high tech library, an IMAX theater, a Blue Angel atrium, a Flight Adventure Deck, a Cubi snack bar and a very professional gift & bookstore. More than 240 volunteers handle the greeting function, security, act as tour guides and take on the important task of restoration of aircraft. The museum had well over 150 historically significant aircraft, a fantastic display of memorabilia, and the largest aviation art collection in the area. The museum was drawing more than a million visitors each year and was listed as one of the top five tourist attractions, along with Disney World, in Florida.

The library was becoming known and continues as one of the premiere holders of historical information on Naval Aviation. The IMAX theater was drawing large crowds to view the Foundation-produced "Magic of Flight," featuring the Blue Angels. The large crowds continue to this day and the "Magic of Flight" is still shown as a premier attraction along with other well-known IMAX productions.

The Blue Angel atrium features four A4D "Skyhawks" hanging two stories up in that world famous Blue Angel diamond formation. It is in this atrium that ceremonial functions such as change of commands, retirements, promotions, and symposiums are held.

The Flight Adventure Deck takes up one whole wing of the museum and is dedicated to the teaching of the mysteries and mechanics of flight to mid-level students. These students come from the schools close to the museum. Two full-time teachers are assigned to the museum by the area school systems and scheduled busloads of students are brought into the museum daily for instructions utilizing the displays and equipment of the Flight Adventure Deck.

The Cubi snack bar is a replica of a famous "watering hole" that was located on the Cubi Naval Station in the Philippine Islands. Over the years literally hundreds of crews from United States' ships and squadrons frequented the Cubi Bar. These crews lined the walls of this establishment with their squadron and ships' plaques and memorabilia, creating a place that became famous throughout the Naval world. The Cubi Naval Station was forced to close when a devastating volcanic eruption covered the base with several feet of volcanic ash. With the closing of the Naval Station, the United States pulled out its presence in this area of the Philippines.

It was decided to rescue all the plaques and memorabilia from the Cubi Bar and transport them to the States where a duplicate bar would be constructed within the Naval Aviation Museum. Detailed photographs were taken of the walls before removal of the plaques and memorabilia for shipment. This was to ensure that each plaque and item would be placed in its correct position on the walls of the duplicate snack bar. The Cubi snack bar, with its Philippine flavor and its walls of history, continues to thrill the many visitors from around the world.

I mentioned the 150 historically significant aircraft above and would like to say here, that the search to find at least one of every kind of aircraft that was ever in the Naval inventory was a joy of life. We found aircraft, or pieces of aircraft that could be restored, in barns, forest, swamps, graves, foreign countries and places it's hard to imagine. The most fruitful place to look for aircraft or remnants of aircraft was under water in lakes and oceans. For instance, we recovered thirty-three World War II and earlier aircraft from Lake Michigan. These were some of the aircraft lost in operation around the two training aircraft carriers that operated in the Great Lakes for many years. It never ceased to amaze me when an aircraft was recovered, even after fifty years under the water the air would still be in the tires. We also found that after the aircraft batteries were removed from these planes and dried out, they would still pull their full twelve volts, as if new. It was always gratifying when we would get one of these planes beautifully restored and on display. Some visitor to the museum would tell us he flew that plane and was the one who crashed landed it into Lake Michigan. This type of event happened on many occasions as pilots checked their logbooks against the bureau numbers of the restored aircraft on display.

The search will continue to find and recover those aircraft that are missing from the Museum's wanted list. Here, I will only list two of those on that list. One is the Brewster F2A "Buffalo" and the other is the TBD "Devastator". A "Devastator" has been located in several fathoms of water in the Atlantic Ocean off the coast of Miami, Florida, but as yet, has not been salvaged. At last word, the Museum was checking with the government of New Zealand to see if they could help in locating a "Buffalo." In years past, New Zealand had acquired some "Buffalos" as their first line fighter aircraft. As I said, the search will continue and our hope is that one day, we will achieve a complete line of historical Naval aircraft.

When I described the "Blue Angel" atrium earlier, I mentioned that our symposiums were held there. The symposiums are a major part of the Foundation's educational mission. Other than the publication of a quarterly *"Foundation"* magazine and a monthly *"Fly By"* newsletter, the Foundation conducts these symposiums throughout the year covering various important subjects. To name only a few, there have been symposiums on the moon landings, with a panel of all the astronauts who landed on the moon, on the combat fighter aces, with a panel of five of the top scoring fighter aces in the Navy and Marine Corps, on the Battle of the Philippine Sea, with a panel of bomber and fighter pilots who took part in the Mariannas Turkey Shoot and the attack on the Japanese Fleet, and a symposium on the Battle of Midway, with a panel of the senior aviators who led the flights that attacked the Japanese Fleet. You can see from this small list that the symposiums cover a broad, important and interesting field and are highly educational.

The names of the moderators and speakers of these symposiums sound like a Who's Who of America. I recall when President George W.H. Bush, the 41st president of the United States, was the speaker at the banquet following one of the symposiums. President Bush was a Lieutenant Junior Grade, Naval Aviator during World War II and fought the war from the deck of the aircraft carrier *USS San Jacinto*. During his speech those in the audience were hanging on every word as he related the tale of being shot down while on a bombing mission against an island in the Iwo Jima chain. He told of landing in the water and his rescue by one of our submarines only a few minutes ahead of an enemy gunboat coming out from the island. He added some comical details of how he, a Naval aviator, was assigned duty as a part of the submarine's crew until they were able to return him to his aviation duty. He also told how many years after the war he had returned to the island where he had been shot down and, to his surprise, found that the people on the island practiced cannibalism. Showing his wit, and to the thrill of the audience, he stated, "Do you know, if that submarine had not been there to pick me up, your president could have been a shish kebab." I can tell you, after that the laughter went on for several minutes. This small, witty story by President Bush is but one of many such stories told by the leaders of industry, military, education, medicine and religion who accept the task of moderators and speakers for the Museum Foundation's sponsored symposiums.

The Foundation's undertaking of the education side of its mission and its accomplishments through the fourth stage of planned construction have been commendable; but we are not through. The fifth stage, the National Flight Academy, is our next goal, and when completed the museum will encompass over

500,000 square feet. The National Flight Academy is planned as a wing of the museum. It will contain equipped classrooms, a dormitory with messing facilities to house and feed over 250 students plus multiple hands-on modules and working displays. The students are envisioned as twelve-year-old boys and girls who sign up and travel to Pensacola for the six-week course. The University of West Florida will furnish enrolled college students to act as leaders for the ten to twelve students who will make up the squadrons. The college student will shepherd his or her squadron through the entire six weeks. The idea of the course is to interest young students in the study of math and science by their hands-on study of aviation and space travel. There will be a nominal charge for the six-week course and the Foundation envisions setting up a fund, with donations from Corporate America, which will provide tuition for those unable to pay.

The Secretary of the Navy has given approval for the establishment of the National Flight Academy and the Foundation has established plans for raising the $36,000,000 to construct and equip the building. The plan calls for a scheduled opening in the 2006 time frame.

It was at this point in time, that my duties as Chief of Staff and Secretary Treasurer of the Foundation, came to a close. I decided that after twenty-five years with the Foundation it was time to move on, pass along my duties, and bring some new blood into the Foundation.

Finally, after fifty-six years of service to the US Navy, in and out of uniform, I was ready to go ashore to live out the rest of my life, content with my memories.

Angel In The Cockpit

Note from Louise Bancroft Hawkins

Shortly after my husband completed the first draft of his book, he died. I was devastated by this loss, but determined to see his book published. It has been a long struggle of dealing with the editing, and assembling of photos, but I believe he would be as proud of the final result, as I am of him.

A measure of the widespread regard for Hawk was exemplified by the following Obituary, picked up by the Associated Press and run in newspapers all across the country.

Captain Arthur Hawkins, 81, Navy flying ace

PENSACOLA, Fla. -- Retired Captain Arthur Ray "Hawk" Hawkins, one of the Navy's top flying aces, died March 21 of complications from a stroke. He was 81

Captain Hawkins was the Navy's 10th-ranking ace during World War II, with 14 confirmed and three probable aerial victories, all while flying F6F Hellcats. He flew from the aircraft carriers USS Cabot and USS Belleau Wood.

Captain Hawkins's war record included destroying 39 aircraft on the ground. His awards included three Navy Cross and two Distinguished Flying Cross medals.

He was inspired to join the Navy at 19 by the 1942 death of his older brother, an Army Air Forces fighter pilot shot down in the South Pacific.

Captain Hawkins was a slot pilot with the Blue Angels acrobatic team from 1948 through 1950 and returned as flight leader in 1952-53. During the latter tour, he became the first person to survive an ejection at supersonic speed.

While stationed in Japan during the Vietnam War, he worked to recover Japanese family artifacts lost during World War II. He was awarded the Emperor of Japan Third Order of the Sacred Treasure, which historians say was the highest award ever given by Japan to a foreign military officer.

Ode to the Hawk

Where, one might ask, is the town of Zavalla
Does it have any claim to fame?
And why, one might add, is it proud of one fella?
And what was the name of his game?

Well, that East Texas town has its hero
who left from that place one day.
At war he made scrap of the zero.
As a Blue he made flight look like play.

Well, who is this guy and why all the talk?
Have we ever heard his story?
You bet we have, his name is Hawk
and he's history covered with glory.

Little more than a lad when he answered the call
he took to the air in fighters.
Before he could vote, he had faced one and all
dispatching fourteen poor blighters.

His great deeds caught the eyes of his bosses
but Hawk wasted no time in his braggin'.
Aerial skill brought him two Navy Crosses
then a third for a cruiser and 'wagon.

War's end found our friend back stateside
a member of the Navy's first team.
He soon was picked for the angels.
He was part of the creme de la creme.

Angel In The Cockpit

Then Korea and another deployment.
To the kittens he lent his name.
Between flights he added enjoyment
by running a floating crap game.

Back with the Angels, they made him the boss.
The team he was told to revive.
His outside loop was the only loss.
He was the first such to survive.

After long years of serving his nation;
after skipper, leader and CAG;
he retired and joined the foundation,
airshows, raising money his bag.

From east to west he'd race to a show.
Through Texas he blazed a new trail.
When the highway patrol saw how fast he could go,
Ole Hawk they would nail without fail.

But the years go by and it's time to rest.
There's nothing more to prove.
He's met every challenge and come out best.
And now it's time for a move

With lovely Louise, take a turn at life's ease
Lord knows, you have it coming.
When you loaf around or drive off the tees,
the rest of us will be bumming.

As you step o'er the side, we're saddened.
We hate to see you leave.
Actually we should be gladdened.
Retirement's not something to grieve.

So, I though of a way to make your day.
And I think you're going to love it.
Tell that guy at your side "it's been a great ride,
but you can take this job and shove it!"